Liz Hodgkinson has been a newspaper and magazine journalist since 1967, specializing for the last few years in the health field. She has written many books including *Smile Therapy*, *Addictions*, *Sex Is Not Compulsory*, *Unholy Matrimony*, *The Alexander Technique* and *How to Banish Cellulite Forever*.

GW00419075

By the same author

LIZ HODGKINSON

THE ANTI-CELLULITE RECIPE BOOK

GRAFTON BOOKS

A Division of the Collins Publishing Group

LONDON GLASGOW
TORONTO SYDNEY AUCKLAND

Grafton Books
A Division of the Collins Publishing Group
8 Grafton Street, London W1X 3LA

A Grafton Paperback Original 1990

A CIP catalogue record for this book is available from the
British Library

ISBN 0-586-21019-9

Printed and bound in Great Britain by
Collins, Glasgow

Set in Electra

CONTENTS

INTRODUCTION

When my first book on cellulite, *How To Banish Cellulite Forever*, was published I confidently expected loud howls of opposition from the medical profession, who have told us for years that there is no such thing as cellulite.

But they never came. Most of the women doctors I spoke to about cellulite said that large numbers of their female patients complained of this condition and asked whether anything could be done about it. Many admitted that they too suffered from a cellulite problem, and would themselves love to know how they could get rid of the lumps and bumps on their thighs.

The male doctors were also far less dismissive than I had expected. As a cellulite 'expert' I was asked to speak on radio and television, often in conjunction with somebody medically qualified. Most of the male doctors whose opinion was canvassed said that although they had heard of cellulite they did not know what it was and there had been no mention of it in their medical training. However, they wanted to find out more, as they knew it was something that bothered many women.

The success of my original book, the sheer number of

patent anti-cellulite remedies now on the market, and the surprisingly positive reaction of the medical profession have combined to convince me that cellulite is finally being taken seriously. Although the word is not an English one – it is a term we have on permanent loan from the French – the condition is all too obvious to hundreds of thousands of women.

Cellulite is the hard, lumpy, bumpy fat that appears on female – although not male – thighs, bottoms and upper arms. It has a 'cottage-cheese' or 'orange-peel' appearance when puckered, and forms dimples and ridges. It is not, strictly speaking, real fat but accumulated waterlogged wastes that have become trapped in fat cells and cannot easily escape.

Although cellulite can affect women of any age it tends to become worse as we grow older, which is why the thighs of so many women in their fifties and sixties and beyond are an unattractive sight. Because cellulite tends to creep up on us with advancing age it has often been assumed that it is as inevitable as grey hair or wrinkles. But it is not. Grey hair and wrinkles are natural physiological changes which we can do little to avoid. Some people get grey hair, if that is their genetic make up, whatever they eat or drink or do. The same applies to wrinkles, and to baldness in men. They are determined mainly by hereditary factors and are largely beyond individual control.

This is not the case with cellulite. The type of waste that becomes trapped in fat cells is not supposed to be there, and has only accumulated because our lifestyle has allowed it to. Cellulite is basically a circulation and water-retention problem, and is a sign that the body is unable to eliminate all its wastes.

It is because of the female hormone oestrogen that only women develop cellulite. Oestrogen does its best to protect vital organs in the event of a pregnancy, so sends toxic wastes that cannot be eliminated through the ordinary channels to out-of-the-way sites where they will be relatively harmless. Once deposited, cellulite can be extremely hard to get rid of because the body behaves as if it has now completed its job of waste disposal.

Women have cellulite, and men have heart attacks. The mechanisms that cause arteries to become clogged with cholesterol deposits, leading to heart attacks, are very similar to those that result in cellulite for women. In both cases, an unhealthy diet, compounded by a sedentary lifestyle and poor circulation, has resulted in the accumulation of dangerous or toxic substances. Obviously excess cholesterol does more harm than cellulite, as it stays around the heart.

Few women feel ill as a result of cellulite, but many feel disgust when they look at their thighs and see puckers and dimples instead of smooth, slim pins. I had two decades of feeling disgusted whenever I caught sight of my thighs but now that I live an anti-cellulite lifestyle I actually like them.

Until recently most women put up with their cellulite because they thought they had no choice in the matter. There was no known way of getting rid of it, apart, perhaps, from succumbing to the horrendous surgical procedure known as liposuction, where excess fat is sucked out under general anaesthetic. However, even liposuction cannot get rid of all the cellulite, although it is undoubtedly successful in reducing fat permanently.

Now, though, we know that there is a safe and guaranteed way of getting rid of cellulite and preventing it from accumulating in future. The regime requires motivation and dedication, and a willingness to change one's diet from an unhealthy to a healthy one. This is most important. Although there are four ingredients to a successful anti-cellulite programme – diet, body brushing, massage and aromatherapy – the last three will not work unless you are prepared to undertake the diet as well. Nor will diet work all by itself for most people. Fat cells are most reluctant to yield up their cellulite deposits, and require the utmost gentle but persistent persuasion.

One moan from many people reading my original book was: 'But what can I eat?' At first glance it seemed that the anti-cellulite diet cut out everything most of us enjoy eating or even regard as essential fare. Bread and dairy products are excluded, as are many convenience foods and products containing added sugar.

The diet looks harder than it actually is because it requires most people to make a complete break from their usual eating habits. In fact, there are very many delicious things that you can eat *and* lose your cellulite, and this book tells you how to prepare a huge variety of anti-cellulite dishes.

I have compiled this book to show cellulite sufferers how easy it is to cut out from their diet everything that encourages the lumps and bumps to form, and to enjoy those foods that work to send the bulges away. Most of the recipes are vegetarian, and can be put together without any great culinary skill. Although, like many people, I enjoy spending a day in the kitchen from time to time, I do not want to spend hours cooking every day. Many of the recipes are ready to eat, from start to finish, in half an hour. Those that take longer just have to be put in the oven to cook.

The recipes are not just for women who wish to be rid of their existing cellulite and prevent any more accumulating. They will also help keep the whole family healthy, help to protect men from heart attacks and children from conditions now thought to be associated with an artificial, dairy-rich diet – hyperactivity, mood swings, tantrums and learning difficulties.

What's more, the whole family will enjoy them, as they are tasty and filling as well as good for you.

PART I

The Anti-Cellulite Diet

CHAPTER ONE

THE IMPORTANCE OF DIET

Since *How To Banish Cellulite Forever* appeared, a lot of patent anti-cellulite treatments have come on to the market. The anti-cellulite business appears to be getting bigger all the time. Most of the new treatments have been brought out by major, multi-national cosmetic houses and introduced with huge amounts of hype and enormous advertising budgets. The treatments promise that diligent application will deliver smooth, bulge-free contours, and this message is underlined by pictures of super-slim models displaying impossibly thin thighs.

True, the word 'cellulite' is rarely mentioned when these products are advertised. 'Cellulite' is a word that is still not officially admitted in respectable cosmetic or medical circles. We hear instead terms like 'body sculpturing' and 'contouring' – the advertisements are very clever indeed.

Most of these creams and lotions containing the results of the 'latest scientific research' are extremely expensive. But do they work? Well, *very* diligent and dedicated long-term use may make some small difference but the truth is that no anti-cellulite cream, lotion or oil can have very much effect unless you are prepared to undertake the anti-cellulite diet as well. Otherwise, as fast as you are sculpturing your body with the aid of the scientifically developed cream you are encouraging new bulges and bumps to form by eating the wrong food. So you will be fighting a guaranteed losing battle.

I am not suggesting that diet is the *only* way to deal with cellulite – indeed, in *How To Banish Cellulite Forever* I explain at length that for most people a fourfold attack is essential. Not only diet, but body brushing, aromatherapy and massage are needed to encourage the body to yield up its long-held cellulite deposits. But an effective anti-cellulite regime must start with diet in order to attack the problem from the inside out rather than the outside in.

It used to be believed that the skin was a completely waterproof covering which nothing could penetrate. We now know that this is not the case, and a whole new range of cosmetics and transdermal drugs – where a patch is applied to the skin and the drug seeps through to the area beneath – has been developed which take advantage of this new finding. Also, the growing popularity of research into essential oils has shown that certain substances applied to the skin can have a definite therapeutic effect on the whole body. A number of NHS hospitals in Britain are now using the science of essential oils for treating chronic and severe pain – with excellent results.

Aromatherapy is of proven value in the fight against cellulite, but it can never be the whole answer. In order to rid yourself of cellulite deposits you have to employ both strategies – diet and aromatherapy – and both require quite a lot of hard work.

Any reputable aromatherapist will tell you that at least

sixty per cent of the effort must come from you, and the most important part of that effort comes with the diet. If you are serious about banishing cellulite forever you must stay on the diet for the rest of your life. Of course, the very rigorous initial regime does not have to be kept up – nor should it, as it does not constitute a long-term balanced diet – but it is important to develop a diet for life that will maintain the body in a detoxified and toned-up condition.

The reason for this is that cellulite is always liable to come back, much as dust is always trying to settle on household objects, and tarnish on silver and brass. You can only keep it away by constant vigilance. That is an uncomfortable but true fact of life about cellulite. Cellulite describes fat cells that have become filled with waterlogged toxic deposits, and it is very stubborn stuff indeed. In fact, it can be so very difficult to get rid of that many fat and obesity experts have declared that it is impossible. They tell us that we just have to accept these awful lumps and bumps as part of being a woman.

That's what I did for twenty years – just assumed that the hard, lumpy deposits were as much a part of me as my ears and eyes. Now that I have straight, bulge-free thighs for the first time in my adult life I know that cellulite is not an inescapable aspect of being a woman but an aberration, something abnormal, something that should not be there.

Nobody should ever feel discouraged. It is perfectly possible to shift cellulite, however long it has been there, if you make up your mind to pay scrupulous attention to your diet. It is now increasingly realized by doctors and scientists that diet plays a far larger part in all aspects of health maintenance than was previously believed. For many years, doctors laughed at the idea that illness could be caused or made worse by diet, and they insisted on telling us that nowadays everybody ate a perfectly balanced, nutritious diet, at least in the West. Those people who suspected that diet might be at the root of their health problems were usually written off as time-wasters and hypochondriacs. Alternative practitioners who tried to treat illnesses by dietary means were dismissed as charlatans and unqualified get-rich-quick merchants.

Now, however, the situation has changed beyond all recognition. Orthodox medical opinion is fast coming round to the view that diet may be a contributory factor to a wide variety of chronic conditions, from arthritis and heart disease to cancer, ME, multiple sclerosis, allergies, asthma, eczema, hyperactivity in children, migraine, irritable bowel syndrome, ulcers, skin disorders, candida albicans, low energy levels, and infertility.

There is increasing evidence that food intolerance is a very real problem, and may be responsible for a wide range of illnesses. It seems that everyday foods such as milk, wheat and sugar could be at the root of poor health in many cases. Allergies, particularly food allergies, are becoming more common all the time, and doctors are having great success in both diagnosing and treating a large number of allergy complaints by diet.

Most people consider that cellulite is not a serious illness. In fact, it is usually not considered an illness at all, and concern over cellulite is often seen as an expression of vanity. With so many problems in the world, how dare women worry about a few lumps and bumps? I am sure one of the reasons so many people – including women – deny the existence of cellulite is that there is a guilty feeling that it is wrong to be so concerned about appearance. After all, even if you have cellulite, you probably do not actually feel unwell from it. And if you are dismayed by the sight of your naked body, well, you just have a negative body image which must be overcome by positive thinking. There is a school of thought that says women should be happy with their bodies whatever shape they are, and should not put themselves at the mercy of cosmetic houses and questionable practitioners who have identified yet another area of women's bodies to worry about. This line of thought says that our present obsession with slimness and eternal youth is media-led, so much nonsense, and that 'real' women have lumps, bumps, wrinkles, grey hair and uneven teeth, so we should not all try to look the same, or attempt to conform to an impossible ideal.

To some extent I go along with these arguments. There is no reason why we should all be exactly the same shape and size, production-line women. We are all made differently, and not everybody is going to be five feet ten and size eight, whatever self-tortures are applied.

However, I also believe that it is easier to love oneself and have a positive body image when one has done one's very best to maintain one's optimum shape and condition. To worry about cellulite is not the same as worrying about a big nose, or thick ankles – it is not merely a cosmetic concern but an actual health problem. I am now convinced of this. Furthermore, although the presence of cellulite may not exactly make you feel ill, you will certainly feel a great deal better about yourself when it has gone. There is no doubt in my mind that my general health improved along with my appearance once I decided to mount a concerted attack on cellulite.

At the same time as my cellulite gradually disappeared – and it took about three months in my case before a real effect was visible – I noticed that I had new energy levels, that I could walk much further without getting tired, and that I felt generally cleaner and less clogged-up inside. So many of us have become used to a less-than-optimum health and energy level that we accept it as normal.

While using myself as a guinea pig I learned a lot about health and nutrition and how my body worked. Before, I had hardly taken any interest, and had just fed it at intervals. Now I am extremely careful about what I eat. My whole system has become more sensitively tuned, and I have started to imagine what might be going on in my body when I have alcohol, butter-covered pasta, coffee and ice-cream all in the same meal. Although this combination is delicious when you are eating it, you don't feel so good afterwards. On the anti-cellulite diet, you will feel good all the time. Added bonuses are that the condition of your skin and hair will improve and you will experience a whole new positive feeling about yourself. Most cellulite sufferers do not feel in the least bit ill – at least not because of their cellulite, because the body has done its very best to transfer toxic wastes to out-of-the-way areas where they will do least harm. But the very existence of cellulite is an indication that not everything is well inside. It is a warning that your body is taking in more waste matter than it can comfortably handle, and that your circulation is sluggish.

Once you start the diet everything speeds up simultaneously. You will notice that transit time – the amount of time food takes to go through the digestive tract and be eliminated from your body – gets faster and that your head feels much clearer.

The anti-cellulite diet is important because it gives the body a chance to detoxify itself so that the cellulite can be eliminated. The reason it has accumulated in the first place is that the body's organs of elimination have too much work to do. The only way to detoxify your body is to eat as many pure, natural substances as possible and cut out all the refined, processed, non-nutritive foods. This gives the lymphatic system – the body's own vacuum cleaner – an opportunity to do its job properly and dispose of toxic substances.

Since my first book on cellulite was published, many people who do not wish to relinquish their bad eating habits have informed me that this or that person eats nothing but Mars bars, gets through thirty cigarettes and a bottle of wine a day, and still has no cellulite. People have told me that most dancers and athletes, some of whom eat a terrible junk-food diet, have not a trace of cellulite.

Well, so they might. And if you haven't got any cellulite, then you can continue eating all the rubbish you like. But if you have, and you wish to get rid of it, you have no choice but to follow the diet. If you have cellulite, and have had it for a long time, you are not going to lose it on a diet of chips, sausages, ice-cream, chocolate, cigarettes and alcohol.

Dancers and athletes do not have cellulite because even though they may eat a terrible diet they are on the move all the time and exercise strenuously. Cellulite does not have a chance to form on them. But these same people often succumb to arthritis in later life, and this is very likely closely connected with the bad diet they ate when in training.

The problem is, the vast majority of women who suffer from cellulite are couch potatoes – as well as eating self-indulgently, they never take any exercise. This was me for twenty years. I have always been a greedy pig over food, and at the same time physically lazy. I smoked and drank and took the contraceptive pill throughout my twenties. I hated exercise, I couldn't bear the thought of Spartan eating regimes. I shared the attitude of Milton's *Comus*

> . . . if all the world
> should in a pet of temperance feed on pulse
> Drink the clear stream and nothing wear but frieze,
> The all-Giver would be unthanked, would be unpraised,
> Not half his riches known and yet despised . . .

Now I have a different attitude. I believe that if all the world did feed on pulses (a wonderful anti-cellulite food, and also good for unfurring the arteries) and drank the clear, unpolluted stream, the world's health would improve enormously and very many of our 'diseases of civilization', as author Brian Inglis has called them, would disappear – including cellulite.

The relationship of diet to cellulite means that the worse the diet, the higher the risk of cellulite deposits. Not everybody who smokes fifty cigarettes a day will die of lung cancer, but they are at high risk. The same with cellulite. The more junk you put in your system, the higher the risk of cellulite will be. You may not succumb – but your chances are not good.

If you have cellulite – and around eighty per cent of Western women have – then it will have been encouraged to form by a combination of a toxic diet, sedentary habits causing poor circulation, and taking in more pollutants of all kinds than your body can comfortably handle. There is also a hereditary factor in cellulite – if your mother has it then your chances of getting it will be high.

Modern processed foods encourage cellulite deposits because the body is not equipped to deal with artificial colours, flavours, pesticides, hormones from dairy produce, and large amounts of refined sugar. So it rebels, in one way or another. One woman may have terrible headaches, while another has cellulite. Men develop beer bellies and suffer heart attacks. Children often become hyperactive. Nobody is immune from the bad effects of an unhealthy diet, and there are many ways that ill health of one sort or another may manifest itself.

Even if we eat a highly nutritious diet we still take in waste products and toxic matter. But if the diet is basically pure and natural the digestive system will be able to cope with any rubbish, sending it to the organs of elimination (the skin, bowels, kidneys and lymphatic system) to be passed out of the body. To facilitate this, the colon contains bacteria which work to break down food particles into a form that can be processed. However, if there is not enough beneficial bacteria in the colon, waste matter becomes re-absorbed into the bloodstream where it can cause a variety of conditions. In women, although not in men, the female hormone oestrogen does its best to make sure these toxic wastes do not go anywhere near vital organs in the event of a pregnancy. So it sends them to the thighs, hips, buttocks and upper arms.

The trouble is, beneficial bacteria are easily killed off by many aspects of modern living, such as antibiotics, high fat and heavy protein diets, high sugar consumption and too little dietary fibre. The anti-cellulite diet, however, will encourage the body's eco-system to return to normal and to eliminate waste matter effectively.

The main purpose of the anti-cellulite diet is to enable the body to detoxify itself by eliminating long-held wastes. It is not a reducing diet as such, although if you are overweight as well it will certainly help you get your weight back to normal.

I cannot overstress the importance of the right diet in an effective anti-cellulite regime. When I first embarked on the programme myself I was highly sceptical and also, if the truth be told, extremely reluctant to give up all the foods I enjoyed – rich cheesecakes, cheesy moussakas, buttery pasta dishes. All these foods are described by nutritionists as 'highly palatable', as they deliver a feeling of fullness and satisfaction. But they don't always do such nice things to your innards. While your are giving your taste buds short-term satisfaction you may be being unkind to your body.

Many women imagine that crinkly, bumpy skin is inevitable as they grow older. But although skin and contours cannot indefinitely keep the smooth, wrinkle-free appearance of youth, cellulite need never be a problem. It's ageing, unsightly and unhealthy, and your outward sign of a sluggish system. Embark on the anti-cellulite diet and you are halfway towards getting rid of it.

CHAPTER TWO

THE PRINCIPLES BEHIND THE DIET

When the basic anti-cellulite diet was first outlined to me I blanched. It sounded impossible, as well as unappetizing. From henceforth, if I seriously wanted to rid my body of those dreaded lumps and bumps I would have to eschew, rather than chew, most of the foods I had come to love over the years – for the rest of my life.

My aromatherapist, Frances Clifford, told me that I should not eat wheat, dairy products, eggs, food with added sugar, chocolate, rice pudding, processed foods, salted nuts, marmalade, jam (even sugar-free kinds), pasta, cakes, biscuits, ice-cream, cheesecake, crisps or ready-prepared snacks or meals. All these, she told me, were cellulite-forming. Moreover, I would have to say good-bye to coffee (which figured largely in my life at that time), tea, cocoa, alcohol, fizzy drinks – low- as well as high-calorie ones – packet soups and sweetened fruit juices – nectars, as they are misleadingly known. The regime sounded the most Spartan, the most self-denying imaginable.

Aargh, I thought, as I contemplated it. Was it, could it, be worth it? More to the point, would I be able to stick to it?

And what guarantee did I have that for weeks of horrible deprivation I would be rewarded by lovely long, slim thighs?

Could all those wonderful foods – fresh, hot wholemeal bread, wonderful steaming coffee, blissful chocolate cake – really be bad for me? Why was it, I asked myself, that all the foods most people enjoy are bad for them, while the 'healthy' ones never set the taste buds tingling or the mouth drooling? The answer was, as I found from researches, that the foods we enjoy so much are the ones we actually crave, the substances that set up addictions in the body and act rather like drugs. Sugar, fats, meats can all be as highly addictive in their way as nicotine and caffeine. The foods that are genuinely health-giving, such as organic fruits and vegetables, rarely set up that reaction. When you've had enough you've had enough, and never develop a craving for more than your body needs.

I asked Frances what I *could* eat and drink. She gave me a list of 'permitted' foods and beverages. The list did not seem all that long. It included all fresh fruits and vegetables, except for large amounts of citrus fruits which apparently the liver finds hard to accommodate, brown rice, oatcakes and barley-cakes, porridge oats, tea and coffee substitutes, herbal teas, carob, pulses, tofu, unsalted nuts (apart from peanuts, which are not really nuts and are as bad as the other forbidden foods), jacket potatoes, and loads of salad with olive oil or vinaigrette. I could also have small amounts of yoghurt, provided it was the live, low-fat variety and not my favourite thick, creamy Greek-type yoghurt. Oh, and lots and lots of mineral water. In fact, I could hardly get enough, Frances said. I could drink eight glasses a day if I wanted to. Gee, thanks.

The anti-cellulite diet, I discovered, was not formulated purely for curing cellulite. It was first suggested by an American dentist, Weston Price, who travelled the world studying the diets of pre-literate societies. He found that the closer to nature their food, the healthier these people stayed. As a dentist, Weston Price was mainly interested in the shape and condition of teeth, and found that in societies where a natural diet was followed, teeth and jaws remained in excellent condition throughout life.

In 1938 he published his book *Nutrition and Physical Degeneration*, a fierce attack on 'degenerate' Western diets, with their refined sugar and flour, and over-treated milk and meat which, he said, were leading to early dental decay and misshapen jaws.

From Dr Weston Price's original researches have developed all the detoxifying and 'natural' diets that have been advocated for restoring health. The famous Pritikin diet, devised by Dr Nathan Pritikin, cuts out just about all fat, sugar, salt and animal products. Until he was forty-three, Pritikin, an engineer, was eating an all-American diet of red meat, ice-cream and alcohol. Then he was told by his doctor that his arteries were badly furred up, his cholesterol levels were dangerously high, and he would have to take drugs for the rest of his life. However, Pritikin devised a diet and exercise programme that would bring his cholesterol levels down to normal and keep them there without the aid of drugs. He gave up tea, coffee, alcohol, animal fats and sugar and ate instead fresh vegetables, whole grains and pulses. He also took up regular exercise and from being overweight and ill, became lean and healthy.

By most people's standards, the Pritikin Diet is very restricted indeed, but there seems little doubt that it can help people back to health. It is basically the diet advocated by the Bristol Cancer Help Centre, which pioneered the 'gentle' method of treatment as opposed to strong drugs and surgery. Dr Alec Forbes, a founder of the Centre and author of several books on the Bristol approach, has said that many cancer patients have found the diet extremely difficult. After having cancer diagnosed, they are often then dismayed to learn that the 'gentle' form of treatment means that they must give up all their favourite foods for ever if they want to recover. Dr Forbes does not underestimate the difficulties of changing to such a radical diet but the point is, the eating plan he developed has proved itself. It is not a guaranteed cancer cure, of course, nothing is, but studies undertaken on people who have been able to follow a low-fat, low-meat, stimulant-free diet have shown that their rates of all illnesses, including heart disease and cancer, are far lower than those of the rest of the population.

The anti-arthritis diet, also based on the Pritikin discoveries, is similarly difficult to follow, as it cuts out all the addictive substances. The theory behind the arthritis diet is that artificial foods are the main cause of joints becoming stiff and painful. The process is rather like the way in which cellulite is formed, in that toxic wastes accumulate and cannot be eliminated. Patricia Davis, who was responsible for introducing a successful anti-cellulite regime into Britain, cured her own early arthritis – developed in her twenties after giving up ballet – entirely by diet. After she discovered that the detoxifying diet cured her arthritis, she began to wonder whether it might work for cellulite, which she found to be a major problem among her clients when she set up in practice as an aromatherapist. She discovered that it did, and for years has recommended it to patients with a cellulite problem.

After I had carried out research to my own satisfaction and found that the anti-cellulite diet was not just a cranky fad newly dreamed up, but had a long and honourable history among avant-garde nutritionists, I decided to give it a try. Surely *all* those experts couldn't be wrong. When Nathan Pritikin was examined by doctors after his death, his arteries were found to be as clear and unclogged as a young child's.

For the first two days on the diet I was to try eating nothing but fresh fruit – as much of it as I liked. The idea was to give my body a chance to detoxify fast. Then for the next two weeks the regime was to be quite strict but would include soups, brown rice and large salads. During these two weeks I could do some simple cooking. Not everything had to be raw, but some raw food had to be eaten at each meal. Raw fruit and vegetables – particularly vegetables – contain many enzymes, minerals and vitamins, and these help the system to unclog itself and release the long-held cellulite. The raw food diet is the basic 'cleansing' regime employed at the stricter health farms. Indeed at one health farm, Shrubland Hall in Norfolk, food is never cooked at all. Everything is eaten raw.

I stuck closely to the diet, eating only fruit for two days and then progressing to the half-raw, half-cooked regime for the next two weeks. I drank no tea or coffee for the whole time. I must say that for those two weeks I felt pretty ill. I suffered from migraines for the first time in my life, I felt disorientated, hunger pangs persisted no matter how many bananas I ate, I had dreams of hot buttered toast, and I felt dreadfully deprived. I went to press conferences and business lunches and amazed my colleagues with the abstemiousness of my appetite. I myself often wondered whether I would be able to stand it.

However, two positive things happened. After the two weeks was over, I found I was getting used to the diet. More than that, I was actually starting to enjoy it. I was finding now that if I did eat large amounts of butter or had a sickly cream cake it left me with a heavy, uncomfortable feeling. The diet was beginning to agree with me, and I was becoming more enthusiastic about it. The other positive thing, of course, was that the cellulite started to disappear. The eating regime, aided by body brushing and the aromatherapy oils, encouraged the fat cells to yield up their long-held cellulite deposits, and the liver began to do its work.

I have now, with occasional lapses, followed the 'anti-cellulite' diet for more than two years, and cannot imagine going back to my old ways of eating. True, I had been vegetarian for more than ten years previously, but I still gorged myself on full-fat cheeses, loads of pasta, and puddings with double cream. Now if I eat that sort of food I can almost feel it clogging me up and weighing me down.

I used to think that the anti-cellulite diet was deprivation of the worst sort. Now I realize that the only reason I felt that way was because I had become addicted to bread and dairy products. Also, much, if not most, of my eating was just habit. Over the years I had developed bad habits, and they had become ingrained until I hardly thought about what I ate any more. It was not so much that I believed these foods were delicious as that I did not think for one moment that I could do without them. Researchers into the comparatively new subject of food intolerance tell us that wheat and milk, two common foods that are found in just about everything we eat these days, are the worst culprits, and the main causes of food intolerance. Many people are intolerant of them, and because of this they crave them. We actually crave the foods our bodies are least able to process.

The reason milk and wheat products contribute to the formation of cellulite is that they are heavy and sticky and encourage the formation of mucus. When mucus forms, the liver and kidneys cannot work to eliminate waste matter, so it stays in the system. Excess mucus forms when you are eating foods that your body cannot really tolerate.

On the anti-cellulite diet, foods are not cooked in oil or butter but are 'stir-fried', or sweated, in water or stock instead. The reason for this is that when heated, oils tend to produce dangerous oxygen particles called free radicals, which do immense harm once inside the body. Basically, there are two types of oxygen circulating in the human body – one useful, the other harmful. The oxygen we breathe consists of two units, chemically known as O_2, and these are fine. But during the oxidation process in the body, these chemical bonds are broken down and the units become O_1 instead. In this form they are unstable, and lonely. Alex Comfort has likened free radicals (you'll have to excuse the sexism), to a man at an international conference without his wife – he'll try to bind, temporarily, to any lone female. If it can, the single oxygen unit will bind to carbon or hydrogen, forming either carbon dioxide or water, both of which are rendered harmless as they are breathed out or excreted. But whenever a unit of oxygen cannot find a unit of carbon or hydrogen to bind to, it starts to wreak havoc throughout the body, causing degeneration of tissues. All kinds of illnesses, from diabetes to heart attacks, sunburn and ulcers are now thought to have a connection with the number of free radicals circulating in the body. The more polluted, un-natural substances we take in, the more opportunity there is for these free oxygen radicals to circulate. Part of the damage they cause is to lay fat cells open to invasion by waterlogged wastes – cellulite – as the radicals work to break down cell walls and render them vulnerable to invasion from enemy substances.

There is no way of getting rid of oxygen radicals. Everybody has them, and they are there all the time. In a good state of health, the body has many mechanisms for getting rid of excess radicals. But the more that are produced, the more difficult they are to disperse. Also, some doctors believe, we are losing our ability to deal with free radicals, and the main reasons for this is that we are eating too many refined and denatured foods.

It is increasingly believed that the only way to restrict the amount of excess radicals is to change to a wholefood, organic diet. This is because wholefoods contain large amounts of useful enzymes which mop up the oxygen radicals. All processing destroys enzymes to some extent.

Excess oxygen radicals are destructive, and cellulite is a sign that your body is struggling to cope with them. Although it can probably do little harm when it is safely locked inside fat cells, the presence of cellulite indicates that your circulation is sluggish and that you are harbouring more waste matter than you can eliminate. There is not a direct connection between free radicals and cellulite, except that anything which is generally bad for the body will encourage more cellulite to form.

Tea and coffee are difficult for many people to relinquish. But both are anti-nutrients and the only reason they seem to make you feel better is that they have a stimulating effect. Coffee in particular can quickly have a toxic effect throughout the body, as it contains large amounts of caffeine. It also encourages the dreaded free radicals to form. In coffee, chemicals known as methylxanthines produce free radicals and also drain the body of vital nutrients such as iron, zinc, calcium and magnesium. Decaffeinated coffee is better but is still not a nutrient, and it still contains substances associated with the degeneration of body tissues.

Alcohol also affects body cells adversely, causing blood vessels in the liver and kidneys to become damaged. The more damaged the liver is through alcohol, the less effective it will be as the body's main detoxifying organ. All cleansing diets without exception cut out alcohol, and on the anti-cellulite regime you should ideally not drink any alcohol for the vital first two weeks. After that, a glass of wine a day, particularly if it is organic, can raise your spirits and will not do your health any harm either. Spirits should continue to be avoided. Like caffeine, alcohol is a potent anti-nutrient, and drives important vitamins and minerals out of the body. The body has to work hard to detoxify alcohol anyway, and any excess tends to end up in fat stores, where it is in danger of adding to the cellulite load.

Smoking also contributes to the formation of cellulite – in fact, some nutritionists go so far as to say that smoking is worse for cellulite formation than either alcohol or caffeine. This is because cigarettes contain a large number of toxins, not just nicotine, which can set up adverse reactions throughout the body. Nicotine and benzo-a-pyrene, the other main chemical contained in tobacco, damage the DNA content of cells and also cause more free radicals to circulate. Smoking also drives out important nutrients from the body.

The basic idea behind the anti-cellulite diet is that it is high in nutritional value and low in all substances that can cause physical degeneration, addictions, cravings and toxic conditions within the body. So it is an extremely healthy diet in any case. You will feel much better on this diet than on the standard modern intake of processed and overcooked foods.

It has recently been said that everybody now knows they should eat more fruit and vegetables, less sugar, fat, particularly animal fats, and drink less coffee and alcohol. However, being aware of what a healthy diet consists of is another matter from actually eating healthily. A recent (1989) survey by the market research firm Taylor Nelson found that the diet of the average British schoolchild is worse than ever, with *fewer* fresh fruits and vegetables being eaten than ten years ago. The diet of the average adult is hardly better; we still do not eat enough fruit and vegetables, and we still rely too much on convenience foods and instant taste sensations.

Convenience foods are the nutritional equivalent of a romantic novel, which may be enjoyable and escapist when you are reading it, but is by no means Good Literature. Chocolate bars and ice-cream are escapist food, delivering only calories and little nutritional value.

The diet recommended in this book has the opposite effect – it feeds and nourishes the body properly. It is the Shakespeare, rather than the Barbara Cartland – of diets perhaps harder work to start with, but ultimately much more rewarding and enjoyable.

For the ultimate in nutrition, your raw materials should be organically grown. A few years ago it would have been pointless to recommend organic foods, as these were extremely expensive and difficult to obtain. Now, however, more supermarkets are specializing in organically grown produce, and the space given over to wholefoods is getting bigger all the time. It has become easy to follow the anti-cellulite diet, and inexpensive as well. The recipes in this book all work out far cheaper than frozen and convenience foods.

And what do they taste like? After all, if the diet doesn't taste good, nobody will stick to it, especially when there is such an abundant choice of more tempting products easily available. When I was testing the recipes I realized that I could not rely simply on my own judgment, so I invited a selection of people to come and try them. They were all pronounced absolutely delicious, even by large men who had no cellulite and never would have any, but who did have vast appetites.

It is basically a matter of retraining your taste buds to enjoy good food instead of nutritionally empty food. As with anything else, it is all too easy to develop lazy, bad habits and all too difficult to inculcate good ones. Substituting good for bad ingrained habits is hard, and requires constant practice. At first, I found that sticking to the diet needed attention, as well as motivation. If I wasn't thinking about it, I could easily slip back into my old ways. The only answer was to make the diet a way of life, which is what it has become.

I can now honestly say that I prefer my anti-cellulite diet – which I no longer regard as specifically anti-cellulite, but protective against all degenerative diseases – to the one I was eating before, and that there have been very many bonuses apart from the loss of the hideous orange-peel flesh.

My skin is softer and more wrinkle-free, my hair remains in good condition even though I now punish it with perms and colours, and my general health remains absolutely A1. When I recently had a medical – my first for over twenty years – the doctor could find nothing wrong with me at all.

I cannot be sure what the exact relation is between my good health and what I eat. What I can say, though, is that my contemporaries who do not eat a good diet are not as healthy or in such good shape. On the other hand, just about everybody I know who does eat a good diet – and really, there aren't all that many of us, not even with the proliferation of diet and health books currently on the market – are in superb shape, men as well. Apart from anything else, a bad diet has an ageing effect. Smoking, drinking and junk foods all accelerate the ageing process mightily, especially past the age of thirty-five.

The anti-cellulite diet detoxifies, purifies, and keeps your innards clean and free from waste matter. And that cannot be bad.

CHAPTER THREE

IS IT HEALTHY? IS IT WELL-BALANCED?

You should not imagine that the anti-cellulite diet is suitable only for those who wish to be rid of the lumps and bumps on their thighs. It is a healthy diet that will benefit everybody who eats it. Although it will very definitely help cellulite to disperse, this is not the only good thing about the diet. It will also give the best possible nutritional protection against ill health and those chronic conditions that are now considered to have a dietary ingredient. Studies in the United States have shown categorically that those on a low-fat, high-fibre diet have far lower incidences of all degenerative diseases than people who eat junk food. The nutrition plan detailed in this book will help hyperactive children, people with allergies, women suffering from PMT, and people who succumb to frequent headaches, anxiety attacks or irritable bowel syndrome. It will also help to protect against heart attacks, cancer and arthritis.

But is it well-balanced? Does it contain enough protein, fats and carbohydrates? The answer is emphatically yes. Whenever people are recommended a low-fat, low-protein intake, they always ask the same question: will I get enough protein?

Strangely enough, nobody ever asks whether a diet of burgers or fried chicken will give them enough of the nutrients they need. I've found that people can even feel nervous of changing to a healthy diet because of what their neighbours or friends might think. They say they don't want to be labelled among the brown-rice-and-sandals brigade. Since the 'green' craze, however, this attitude is mercifully disappearing, even among the worst dietary diehards.

In the West, there is no danger whatever of anybody going short of protein or fat. In fact, most people eat far too much of both, with disastrous consequences for their health. Most of us have grown up with the idea that protein is the most important dietary requirement, and that this is mainly supplied in the form of meat, fish, and dairy products such as eggs and cheese. In fact, anti-cellulite recipes exclude these items wherever possible. You will not find a single egg or cheese recipe in the whole book, except for a few instances where low-fat cheeses such as cottage cheese or quark are recommended.

Most of us have heard that meat and fish provide first-class protein whereas vegetable products provide only a second-class version. Therefore, people wonder, how do vegetarians make up this deficiency?

Proteins consist of long chains of amino acids, chemicals that are vital for body growth, maintenance and repair. Some amino acids are 'essential' and can only be supplied through the diet. Most meats and fish provide all the essential amino acids required, whereas vegetable products do not. Foods that deliver the eight essential amino acids are known as complete proteins, whereas foods that provide only some are known as incomplete proteins. Vegetable products are incomplete proteins.

But that does not mean you cannot obtain all your protein requirements from plant foods alone. You can, so long as you make sure you have enough variety. A dish of brown rice and beans will make a complete protein, as together these foods deliver all of the eight essential amino acids. Nuts and rice, or nuts and vegetables together, also make up a complete protein. Baked beans on wholemeal toast are a complete protein.

Most modern slimming diets are low in fat, and some do not have any fat in them at all. However, although most of us in the West eat far too much fat – around forty per cent of the average adult diet consists of fat – we do need some. Fats are necessary for energy, for protection against many diseases and for the synthesis of essential chemicals and hormones in the body. A certain amount of fat is also required for smooth skin, shining hair and strong nails. So the anti-cellulite diet is by no means fat-free.

Yet there is no butter or margarine in any of the recipes. The reason for this is our old enemies, free radicals. When vegetables or meats are fried in fat, huge amounts of free radicals tend to be released. Also, when cooking in oil or fat, you are probably taking in more fat than you realize. We can obtain all the fat we need from unsalted nuts, avocados, and salad dressings made from extra-virgin cold-pressed olive oil. Many of the recipes in this book use oil for dips and dressings, but the fats are not cooked or heated.

The fats used in the anti-cellulite diet are mono-unsaturated, which means they are unlikely to release free radicals into the system. I do not want to enter into a butter-versus-margarine debate here, except to say that, as a general rule, I favour the foods that have been around for thousands of years and have had time to prove themselves, rather than modern laboratory concoctions that contain artificial ingredients. I would rather use small amounts of butter than margarine, and olive oil rather than anonymous 'vegetable' oils which may have been highly processed. My guideline is: the closer to nature, the better. Butter itself is not a highly processed food, although I am wary of it to some extent because the cows may have been fed on all sorts of hormones and antibiotics, and the milk itself will probably have been treated and pasteurized. Cold-pressed olive oil, dark green in colour and with a satisfying sediment at the bottom, has simply been pressed from the raw material – olives – and is as near to nature as any fat can be.

I used to be a real butter and cream freak. Now, I hardly ever buy butter, and instead I use sesame seed and sunflower seed spreads. If you have children, try giving them natural, unsalted, untreated peanut butter without colourings or additives. All children like it, and it is better for them than butter. Instead of buying double or clotted cream, which I used to delight in, I now make my own nut creams with cashews or almonds, liquidized with water, a little honey and natural vanilla essence. They are wonderful – and go down a treat with visitors.

No one actually needs animal fats, in any shape or form. They are all highly saturated, which means in technical terms that the bonds between the carbon atoms that make up the fat are saturated with hydrogen atoms. These fats are not

essential for health or nutrition in any way, although poly-
unsaturated and monounsaturated fats are. Many fats needed
by the body can be made up from other foods, such as
complex carbohydrates. One reason the anti-cellulite diet
contains hardly any meat is because up to eighty per cent of
the calories in many meats are derived from fat. Pork and
beef are the most fat-laden, and even eggs are sixty-six per
cent fat.

The other main macronutrient, carbohydrate, is also
essential for health. In the old days, slimming diets were low
in carbohydrates, and recommended minimal intakes of
potatoes, bread, pasta and rice. We now have a different
approach and believe that complex carbohydrates – that is,
carbohydrates derived from whole sources – are an essential
nutrient. Complex carbohydrates, which contain sugars in a
chemically complex form, are better than simple, or refined,
carbohydrates such as white sugar, because they are slow-
release foods, making them a good source of stamina and
continued energy.

The more you cook carbohydrate-rich foods, the more
chance there is of the starch content being broken down, so
that the sugar enters the blood stream too quickly. Complex
carbohydrates are also a good source of fibre, which is
essential for the quick transit of food through the digestive
system.

There are two main kinds of fibre, soluble and insoluble.
Wheat and wheat products are mainly composed of insoluble
fibre, whereas oat products consist of the soluble kind. This
means they have a greater ability to absorb and help to
eliminate waste matter. So wherever possible you should eat

oat cereals in preference to wheat-based ones, and unsweetened oatcakes rather than biscuits or bread. Oat germ and oat bran can be sprinkled on soups or cereals instead of wheat bran.

Does the anti-cellulite diet provide enough vitamins and minerals? Yes, it does. I take no supplements of any kind and have been perfectly healthy for very many years without needing vitamin or mineral pills. There is some evidence that without meat you may go short of vitamin B12, which is hard to find in sufficient quantity in vegetable products. However, some nutritionists say that the body seems easily able to make up the deficiency without any problem. In any case, the main health risk from the standard diet now eaten in the West is not malnutrition from undereating but from eating too much of the wrong food.

I can already hear another objection. But isn't this diet boring and tedious? Won't you get awfully tired of it? No, not at all. Since you have to try harder to make the meals interesting, you actually get more variety than on a standard meat-and-two-vegetables diet. Also, the meals are far tastier. After all, what could be more boring than a grilled lamb chop, with its two teaspoonsful of meat content? Most meats are extremely boring to eat although, like other high-fat foods such as cheese, they do fill you up fast. The recipes in this book are not only highly nutritious, they are colourful and interesting as well. Many taste sensations in the diet are derived from eating foods that are interestingly spiced and lightly cooked. The recipes are low in salt, but do contain some. How much you add is really up to you, but they should not be oversalted like tinned soups and many prepared convenience dishes. In fact, after a few weeks on the anti-cellulite recipes, most bought processed foods will start to taste too salty.

Although there is no refined sugar in the recipes, a few contain raw sugar or organic honey. There is nothing wrong with eating these foods in extreme moderation, as in their unrefined state they contain some useful nutrients. You have to be careful, though, even with these, as there is addiction potential from all sugars. This is because they enter the bloodstream very quickly and deliver a drug-like 'high', which is then followed by a 'low', making you feel hungry and depressed.

The recipes in this book make you feel satisfied – and keep you satisfied for hours. It is not an exaggeration to say that you will feel a very different person if you make this your diet for life. The advantages of the diet include an end to severe mood swings, food-induced headaches and digestive problems. Not only will you look far better, you will feel much happier and livelier as well.

CHAPTER FOUR

HOW LONG WILL IT TAKE?

The question everybody contemplating the anti-cellulite diet asks is: how long will it take to achieve results?

It would be wonderful if we could diet for one, or at the most two, days and then all the cellulite would be gone for ever. Unfortunately, it does not happen like that. For most people, cellulite deposits have built up gradually over the years and, having lodged themselves firmly in position, are most reluctant to disappear. That is why a dedicated and prolonged attack is necessary, and why you must establish a way of eating that will mean your cellulite does not stand a chance of coming back.

The length of time it will take you to rid your body of cellulite depends on many factors: how long the cellulite has been there, how dedicated you are to persisting with the diet as well as the other aspects – body brushing, aromatherapy and massage – and how much cellulite you have in the first place. No two people's metabolism is the same, and what works for one person will not necessarily have the same result in another.

For some very lucky people, cellulite disappears extremely quickly once they start the regime. In my case, it took a long time – about three months altogether. I didn't notice any real improvement until I had not only been on the diet, but also body-brushed rigorously and massaged with the correct aromatherapy oils for two months. However, once things began to happen, progress was rapid. Everybody noticed that there was something different about me, although of course they did not always know what it was.

For anyone who has had a cellulite problem for five years or more, two months is a reasonable length of time to wait before results become noticeable. For young women who have only just noticed puckers and dimples, a couple of weeks may make an appreciable difference.

It is most important to give your body a really good opportunity to yield up long-held cellulite, so you should stick to the cleansing diet for two weeks if you possibly can. This means no coffee or tea, no cream, cheese or other dairy products, no bread with gluten, no processed or prepared foods, nothing burnt, sautéed or fried, no frozen puddings, ice-cream, desserts, sugar, sweets, chocolate, alcohol or cigarettes.

This list seems endlessly long, but all the items above are definitely not cleansing ones – just the opposite in fact. You should, if you can manage it, have two or three days on fresh fruit alone. At the same time, drink as much mineral water as you can manage – eight glasses a day is not too much.

Fruit and vegetable juices are also good for you, but they need to be diluted and – it should go without saying – not sweetened in any way. Carrot and tomato juice, mixed vegetable juices, pineapple and apple juice will all help the cleansing process.

Unless you have a cast-iron constitution you will most probably find that you do not feel very well when first starting the diet. Don't make this an excuse to return to your bad old eating habits. Feelings of disorientation, headaches, stomach pains are an indication that the regime is working. The symptoms will pass and leave you feeling wonderfully clear and refreshed. You will actually feel cleaned out.

Those who are addicted to tea and coffee will find all this very difficult at first. I was, without realizing it, completely hooked on these drinks, and experienced very severe withdrawal symptoms, so bad in fact that I couldn't work and had to lie down. I had very bad migraines, although I had never suffered from migraines before. But of course, they didn't last and after a day or two they completely disappeared. Now I can exist quite happily on one cup of coffee and one cup of tea a day. All my other drinks are of the non-stimulant variety.

Cellulite sufferers who smoke, drink and eat lots of meat, sugar and dairy products will have the hardest time, as there is so much to relinquish all at once. For these people, it is best to proceed gradually. It will be too hard to give up all your props immediately, so start with the worst culprit first – the nicotine. If you can give up smoking after having been addicted for years, you will definitely feel like a different person, and will be encouraged to make other health-promoting changes in your life.

Coffee and tea are also extremely hard to give up. It is not just that we might be addicted to them, but that very often they are the only drinks on offer. Few restaurants serve herbal tea, and I have never seen coffee substitutes on a menu, except in the very few vegan restaurants that exist. Also, the invitation to 'have a cup of coffee' sounds so harmless and ordinary that we do not always realize what an addictive drug it is. It is probably best to try and cut down on coffee and tea gradually, substituting other drinks for them. If you drink lots of mineral water and fruit juices you will not miss coffee and tea so much.

Sugar is also extremely addictive, which is why we eat so much of it. Sugar addicts may find their favourite fix as difficult to give up as smokers do with tobacco. Whatever you do, don't move on to artificial sweeteners. Although they are very low in calories they will not help with the cellulite problem, as their very artificiality adds to the toxic load on the body. If you simply cannot do without sugar, try substituting organic honey in your drinks. It is just as sweet, but has more nutrients. From a purely nutritional point of view, you do not need added sugar. All fruits and vegetables contain large amounts of natural sugar in a form that the body can easily process.

Don't forget that meat, too, can be highly addictive food. It is one of the reasons it is so popular and people tend to feel deprived when they cannot have it. But meat is actually one of the easiest things to relinquish. Most people simply do not miss it after a while, so long as their meals are tasty, nutritious and filling without it. There is no harm in eating some meat, but you do not need it every day. Simple grilled or baked fish is an acceptable substitute.

The anti-cellulite diet has to be a diet for life. Otherwise, your cellulite will reappear and all your hard work will be wasted. Remember that cellulite is always trying to return and will take up residence again at the slightest provocation. Of course, there is no harm in the occasional indulgence in an ice-cream, a cream cake, or lasagne, but these should never again become part of your staple diet.

Unfair? Well, after two decades of cellulite-laden legs I can say that the diet and the rest of the anti-cellulite regime are absolutely worth it. Of course, I do occasionally miss the treats I used to eat with such relish – huge mounds of spaghetti with lots of greasy sauce, cheesecake with double cream, macaroni cheese, hot toast soaked in oodles of unsalted butter. But I'd rather have slim, cellulite-free legs and excellent health than give way to these momentary taste satisfactions. It is a choice I have to make. Not all of us have to – there are people who eat and drink all sorts of rubbish and never have a trace of cellulite. But it is no use wishing things were otherwise; if you have a propensity to cellulite then the diet is essential for you.

PART II

The Recipes

CHAPTER FIVE

INTRODUCTION TO THE RECIPES

The best anti-cellulite diet is a strictly vegetarian one, where no animal products, including dairy products, are eaten at all. This is why I have devoted a special section to vegetarian meals. But apart from their general 'healthiness', vegetarian meals have several advantages over meat dishes. They are often quicker and easier to prepare and the ingredients are nicer to handle. They tend to be cheaper but, most important, *people enjoy them more!*

When I was first changing from being a carnivore to a vegetarian I often cooked two dishes, one non-meat and one containing meat, for dinner parties. I soon noticed that on every occasion the vegetarian dish disappeared within minutes and the meat dish was left. And my guests were by no means all vegetarian.

Vegetarian meals taste cleaner and lighter than meat ones, and are easier to digest. They don't leave a heavy feeling in the stomach, and many people find they have far more energy on a vegetarian diet.

However, for some people a sudden change to total vegetarianism is neither possible nor desirable. So I have included some anti-cellulite meat and fish dishes at the end of this section. They have been devised by Frances Clifford, the aromatherapist who helped me rid my thighs of the dread bulges and lumps, and who says she is nearly, but not quite, vegetarian herself. The more vegetarian meals you can introduce to your family the better it will be for them, as well as for you. If you do not want to eat meat or fish yourself but the rest of the family does, you can always cook lamb chops, chicken legs or sausages separately for them (or get some carnivore in the family to take responsibility for the meat ingredients).

The one golden rule on any anti-cellulite regime is: no high-fat dairy products. This means no eggs, double cream, full-cream milk, butter, or full-fat cheese. The only permissible dairy foods are low-fat yoghurt and quark, which can be eaten occasionally. You can even replace low-fat yoghurt with soya yoghurt, which in cooked food tastes exactly the same as the dairy variety. The reason for avoiding dairy products is that they are mucus-forming, which means they encourage cells and arteries to become clogged and blocked. Dairy products discourage quick through-put and elimination of food. Another factor is that these days many dairy foods are produced intensively, with the addition of hormones and chemicals, and these encourage the formation of cellulite.

Again, with several of the recipes other members of the family can add their own cheese or butter afterwards if they like.

The other important aspect of anti-cellulite cooking is that, as far as possible, you should not fry in oil or butter. This is in order to avoid the formation of free radicals.

Oils should preferably be monounsaturated, such as olive or rapeseed oil. Do not use artificially produced margarines if you can help it. A very small amount of butter does no harm, as long as you do not use it in cooking.

It is a culinary cliché that vegetables need to be sautéed first. However, this is done out of habit rather than necessity. For years I automatically stir-fried and sautéed everything, because this is what my vegetarian cookery books told me to do. When I started researching the recipes for this book I 'stir-fried' in water or stock instead, and found that the taste was just as good, if not better. The realization that vegetarian cookery does not need initial sautéeing was a revelation to me. When I served up dishes cooked in the new way, nobody noticed, and many were pronounced extra delicious.

Note: The quantities given in these recipes are for four people. But as this kind of cookery is not an exact science the quantities do not need to be followed exactly, especially with the vegetables. Spices are mainly a matter of taste, but err on the mean side at first, especially if the most exotic ingredients are new to you. In any case, anti-cellulite food should not be too highly spiced. Fresh herbs, which are now stocked by supermarkets should be bought in preference to dried, but as busy people do not always have time to shop for fresh herbs at every meal, quantities for dried equivalents are given as well, where appropriate.

CHAPTER SIX

THE ANTI-CELLULITE KITCHEN

Not so very long ago, it would have been quite difficult to obtain the kind of store-cupboard items that are essential for an anti-cellulite kitchen. Now it is easy. The raw materials needed for this healthy way of cooking and eating are widely available from supermarkets and healthfood shops, and also, increasingly, from corner shops. The Indian revolution in corner shops has meant that so many previously exotic or difficult-to-obtain foods are now on sale in practically every town.

When establishing an anti-cellulite kitchen, the emphasis is on natural, additive-free, non-artificially coloured ingredients. Wherever possible, buy the real thing. Do not, for instance, buy instant coffee, but instead keep coffee beans in the freezer and grind them as you require them. It is now possible to buy decaffeinated beans, and also ready-ground decaffeinated filter coffee. The Nairobi Coffee Company produces a water-method decaffeinated filter coffee, in which the caffeine is flushed out of the beans with water. Instead of ordinary Indian tea, buy Luaka, in the mauve packet, which is real tea but low in tannin.

Get into the habit of buying herbal teas. There is now a

huge variety available, so these drinks need never become boring. Invest in a water filter, too, which will soon save you money on bottles of mineral water. However, as no water filter yet delivers sparkling water you will still have to buy this.

All fruit and vegetable juices are good for you, so long as they do not contain added sugar. Always have a big bowl of fresh fruit and lots of fresh vegetables, preferably organically grown. All sprouted grains – alfalfa, mung, beansprouts etc – are good, but they go off very quickly indeed and should really be eaten the same day they are bought.

Buy soya or oat flour instead of wheat flour, and try carob powder instead of chocolate. Carob is rather like chocolate in taste, but is much lower in fat and sugar and is not addictive.

Your store cupboard should always contain seeds and unsalted nuts. Choose from sesame, pumpkin, poppy, caraway and sunflower seeds, pine kernels, almonds, brazils, cashews, chestnuts, walnuts, hazelnuts and pecans. Always buy fresh rather than salted nuts. Peanuts are not recommended on the anti-cellulite diet as they are acid-forming and heavy on the liver.

Keep on the look-out for bread and similar products that do not contain gluten. Rye bread, oatcakes, pumpernickel, barleycakes and puffed rice cakes are all good substitutes for bread.

Always buy brown rice rather than white and buckwheat spaghetti rather than the ordinary kind. Barley can be used in all brown rice recipes for a change.

Do stock up on pulses. Lentils – red, green and brown – do not need soaking so they are worth buying in packets, but if you prefer you can buy tins of the other pulses – butter beans, chick peas, kidney beans etc – to save time. Generally I do not recommend tinned foods, but pulses other than lentils take ages to cook and seem to lose very little in the tinning process. Tins of chick peas and kidney beans are cheap and ready to use, and can be rinsed and added to any salad dish to make a satisfying meal.

Dairy products should be avoided as much as possible. Instead, get into the habit of buying soya milk and tofu – an unfermented soya-bean curd. Soya milk keeps for several months until opened, after which it must be treated like ordinary milk. Plamil and Granose are the big names to look out for in soya products. Granose also make a range of baby foods.

The only yoghurt you should buy from now on is low-fat live plain yoghurt. This is very low in calories and also quite thick. Don't buy any cream – double, single, clotted or sour. Cow's milk should be skimmed or semi-skimmed. Plain cottage cheese, fromage frais, quark – a tasty soft cheese prepared with skimmed milk – and medium-fat vegetable rennet feta are the only acceptable cheeses from now on. Soya cheese, available from healthfood shops, is quite delicious and okay to use occasionally. Prewett's make a reduced-fat cheese, and you can obtain sunflower cheese as well.

Butter is better than margarine, simply because it's more natural and not highly processed. Always buy the unsalted kind, and use extremely sparingly. Do not use in cooking. The vegetable oils you use should be cold-pressed. Always use extra-virgin cold-pressed olive oil, sesame seed, grapeseed, sunflower or safflower oil. Olive oil has a strong taste, whereas sesame seed oil has hardly any taste at all, and so may be better in some recipes where the taste of olive oil is not really wanted.

There are no recipes in this book for eggs. I have not eaten eggs for ten years and have not missed them once. They are not necessary to your diet at all. But if you like them, it goes without saying that any you buy should be free-range, from hens that have been fed on organic produce.

Any meat, fish or poultry you buy should be from an organic source. You do not need meat or fish, but if you like it, or feel you cannot do without it, then eat it from time to time. Smoked meats, fish and cheese are OUT, because the smoking process results in free radicals.

Seasonings are of course extremely important in the anti-cellulite diet. Always buy sea salt and whole peppercorns. Keep a large supply of vegetable stock cubes or buy Vecon or Vegemite in jars. Fresh ginger root is used a lot in the recipes, as is garlic. I have discovered onion powder available from many supermarkets, for dips and pâtés, and it is wonderful. It does not contain any additives, and it saves having to be in floods of tears from chopping up onions all the time.

All the curry spices – turmeric, cumin, coriander, fenugreek, garam masala – are useful, especially when you are cooking low-salt recipes. Cinnamon, allspice, bay leaves, cloves, cayenne, dill, fennel, nutmeg, oregano, paprika, mustard seeds are all vital. Whenever possible, buy herbs such as basil, parsley, coriander, rosemary, sage and thyme fresh. Or grow them yourself, but keep the dried ones handy in case you run out – they're better than nothing.

All flavourings, such as vanilla essence, should be the real thing and not artificial substitutes. It is now becoming far easier to buy real essences. For a long time, only artificial versions were available – I can't imagine why.

Low-salt soya sauce is very handy as a flavouring. You can now also buy 'healthy' versions of tomato ketchup and Worcestershire sauce from healthfood shops.

Spreads and jams should not contain added sugar. I have grown to love sesame seed spread – tahini – and sunflower spread, which I now buy in preference to butter. Whole Earth jams and marmalades do not contain sugar but are quite sweet enough.

You will need a few gadgets, although these recipes do not require many at all: a coffee grinder is very useful for grinding up nuts as well as coffee beans, and a liquidizer is absolutely essential for many of the recipes. A fully fledged food processor is a good idea. Saucepans should not be made of aluminium. A steamer would be useful but is not essential. A garlic press is very useful too. An accurate pair of kitchen scales would help, but most of the recipes do not depend on absolutely accurate amounts.

There is no need whatever to count calories with these recipes. Although they are not all low-calorie, they will certainly discourage fat deposits from forming. They will leave you feeling pleasantly full and satisfied. It is not so easy to overeat brown rice as it is to gorge on pasta with cream sauces.

Convenience foods are not totally forbidden. I stock up on vegetarian sausages, celery burgers, soya frankfurters, soya and mushroom burgers, and nut and sesame burgers. These are all made by Granose and are absolutely delicious. The Realeat company sells vegeburger mixes, soups and ready-made burgers. The instructions are for frying, but I heat them up in the microwave and they are just as nice, if not nicer. They are already cooked and, unlike meat burgers, it doesn't matter all that much if you do not heat them up.

If you have a freezer you can stock up on non-dairy ice-creams – I don't mean those made with whale oil or whatever, but soya frozen desserts. They taste almost the same as 'real' ice-cream, but without the fat content. Also it's a good idea to have frozen vegeburgers and sausages in the freezer for emergencies.

Over the past few years supermarkets have introduced ready-prepared salads. Marks and Spencer do a large range, as do Waitrose and Sainsbury's. These are very useful for those occasions when you do not have time to buy ingredients and chop them up. Most supermarkets now do very imaginative raw vegetable mixes, and although they may seem expensive they can work out cheaper than buying lots of salad ingredients you will only end up throwing away.

All the recipes in this book are easy to prepare. There are no recipes for pastry, cakes, biscuits, bread, soufflés or roulades, for example. The emphasis is on dishes that are easy and quick to cook as well as appetizing and enjoyable to eat.

CHAPTER SEVEN

BREAKFAST

It is often said that breakfast is the most important meal of the day and it is certainly the one I enjoy most. There is plenty of scope for the anti-cellulite breakfast to be both varied and delicious – and filling and satisfying at the same time.

Some people find they can start the day happily with a couple of bananas, and that these will keep them going throughout the morning. This sort of fare will not do at all for me, as I do not find it particularly filling. However, this is the time of day when you can eat a lot of fruit. Nathan Pritikin said that the liver likes fruit until lunch time, and this seems to have been confirmed by later researches. Eat most of your fruit in the morning; the later in the day you eat it, the harder your body finds it to digest.

If you are just starting the anti-cellulite regime, it is best to stick to one variety of fruit at a time rather than having a fruit cocktail, which can be hard work for the digestive system as all the fruits contain different substances. Although slimming diets commonly suggest starting the day with a grapefruit, most anti-cellulite experts do not recommend too much citrus fruit as the liver finds it quite hard to cope with. Grapefruit and oranges are very strong, and in addition contain large amounts of salicylic acid, the aspirin-like chemical that can lead to allergies. Most people find, however, that lemon juice does not cause these problems.

The fruit you eat can be as exotic as you like. Fruits such as papaya, guava, mango, pineapple, passion fruit, persimmon and melon are all wonderful at breakfast time. For a fairly substantial breakfast, grind up in a coffee grinder equal amounts of sunflower, pumpkin and sesame seeds and sprinkle these on the fruit. That will help to keep hunger pangs at bay for a little longer.

You can also keep whole sunflower and pumpkin seeds handy for snacks later during the day. It has been said that sunflower seeds help to reduce a craving for cigarettes, so if you are desperately trying to give up smoking, buy loads of sunflower seeds and have these instead.

Do try not to eat ordinary bread while on the strict anti-cellulite regime, and certainly don't have toast, butter and marmalade. Although for many people this is the standard British breakfast, it could not be worse from a cellulite point of view. First you have the bread, which contains gluten. This tends to clog up the intestines and can cause digestive problems. Then you compound the damage by toasting the bread, thus releasing free radicals. After that you spread on mucus-clogging butter and lastly, sugar-laden jam or marmalade. All in all, a highly processed and not very healthy start to the day.

It can be hard to persist with fruit and mineral water while everybody else is feasting on highly palatable breakfasts, but it will be worth it in the end. You will come to look forward to this light, energizing start to the day.

It is a good idea to get into the habit of not drinking at the same time as you are eating, as liquids tend to dilute the digestive juices, making it harder to digest food properly. When you first wake up, have a glass of mineral water or a wake-up herbal tea but do not drink with your breakfast.

You should not drink tea or coffee for the first two weeks of the anti-cellulite diet. Instead, have herbal tea or a coffee substitute. For a long time, I could not find any decent coffee substitutes, but now I have come across two that are really quite acceptable – Aromalt and Yannoh, both widely available from healthfood shops. No coffee substitute has quite the taste of the real thing, of course, but all serious cellulite-shifters must try to wean themselves off caffeine.

You can drink decaffeinated coffee so long as the caffeine has been removed by the water process – if it has, it will say so on the packet. Otherwise, you are just substituting one set of chemicals for other chemicals, which are probably just as harmful in their way.

Any cow's milk you buy should be skimmed or semi-skimmed. I now find that full-fat milk is too rich for me, and the skimmed variety is just right. So much of what we think we like is purely the result of ingrained habit, rather than absolute free choice.

If you possibly can, try to exist on fruit alone, or fruit plus ground natural seeds, for breakfast for a week. Then you can introduce more substantial fare, such as porridge, muesli and yoghurt-based shakes.

Porridge is a very good, healthy food for all the family, provided it is made in the traditional way, and not with lashings of milk, cream and sugar. You can add a small amount of organic honey, chopped dates or figs, or soaked Hunza apricots to the basic oat mixture. To make porridge, use twice the amount of water to porridge oats, bring to the boil then simmer, stirring all the time, until you have a smooth paste.

Muesli is also a good choice for breakfast, so long as it does not contain added sugar or any preservatives or additives. Many readymade mueslis are very high in both fats and sugar, so read the label carefully first. Soak overnight in a little mineral water and then eat with live low-fat yoghurt in the morning.

One of my favourite breakfasts is a banana shake, quickly made in the liquidizer. All you do is empty the contents of a small carton of low-fat yoghurt (use soya yoghurt if you prefer) into the liquidizer, chop up a banana and add that, together with a squeeze of lemon juice and half a teaspoon of organic honey. Blend well until all is smooth, then serve topped with ground nuts. Or you could add a few dates, figs or soaked apricots.

You do not necessarily have to give up bread at the start of the day. Oatcakes, pumpernickel, rye and Manna bread (a sprouted, unleavened bread made without added salt, sugar or preservatives) are all acceptable gluten-free substitutes, or you can buy special gluten-free bread, which is now quite widely available. Oatcakes with sesame or sunflower seed spread will last just as long as hot buttered toast and marmalade, and once you have got used to them you may even find you prefer them. I do, now. Wholemeal pitta bread, which is unleavened, can be heated in the oven or microwave and then filled with sesame or sunflower spread.

If you must have jam or marmalade, try the Whole Earth varieties, which do not contain any sugar, although they are still high in calories.

Whatever you do, never go without breakfast. There is always the danger of snacking on junk food in the middle of the morning, and then making yourself feel horrible as a result. Breakfast need only take a very few minutes to prepare and eat, and it will set you up for hours. It is especially important to have a nutritious, non-cellulite-forming breakfast if you work in a place where you cannot easily get the right sort of food at lunch time. Staff canteens, school and college dining halls and sandwich bars are unlikely to be able to provide the kind of food you should ideally be eating. It is a good idea to take herbal tea bags and a coffee substitute into work, so that you do not succumb to the tealady's offerings.

CHAPTER EIGHT

SOUPS

These soups are quick and easy to make. Unlike most recipes for soups, they do not rely on initial sautéeing in oil or butter. You may notice that they taste slightly different from the homemade soups you are used to, and the difference will be that they are lighter and fresher in taste.

The fresher the vegetables, the tastier the soups will be. These ones require little or no culinary skill, but most do need a food processor or liquidizer. Some people quite like soups with bits of vegetables swimming around in them – I prefer mine to be smooth.

Anyone just starting an anti-cellulite regime can safely eat all the soups here. If they are not quite filling enough you can always sprinkle on top a mixture of ground sunflower, sesame and pumpkin seeds. In fact, you should always keep a jar of this mixture handy to sprinkle over vegetables and soups, as it will stop you going for the bread and butter.

Chestnut Soup

This soup has a rather 'Christmassy' taste, but of course it can be eaten at any time of the year. It's very nutritious and filling, and extremely 'more-ish'.

6oz (175g) tinned or dried chestnuts – dried ones will need soaking overnight
2 onions, chopped
2 carrots, finely chopped
2 sticks celery, chopped
½ teaspoon fresh thyme, or ¼ teaspoon dried
about ¼ nutmeg, grated
sea salt and freshly ground black pepper
1–1½ pints (600–900ml) vegetable stock (for tinned chestnuts, otherwise use 2 pints (1.2l) water)
2 tablespoons chopped fresh parsley

Preparation time: 10 minutes
Cooking time: if using tinned chestnuts, about 45 minutes; otherwise 1½ hours. Note: with dried chestnuts you have to think about this recipe 24 hours in advance.

If using dried chestnuts, put in a bowl and pour over 2 pints (1.2l) boiling water. Leave to soak for 24 hours, then put the chestnuts plus the soaking liquid in a large saucepan and add the onions, carrots and celery. Bring to the boil. If using tinned chestnuts, bring to the boil with the vegetable stock instead of water. Cover and simmer until tender – wait 1½ hours for dried chestnuts, 30 minutes for tinned. Allow to cool slightly, then liquidize. Return to the saucepan, and reheat gently with the thyme, nutmeg and seasoning. Do not allow to boil again. If the mixture is too thick, add more stock or water. Garnish with the parsley to serve.

Leek and Potato Soup

A quick, easy and satisfying soup for when leeks are in season.

1 medium onion, finely chopped
2 large leeks, washed and chopped
2 large potatoes, scrubbed and cubed
2oz (50g) ground cashews or hazelnuts
1 pint (600ml) vegetable stock
pinch mixed dried herbs
sea salt and freshly ground black pepper

Preparation time: 10 minutes
Cooking time: 35 minutes

Heat 2–3 tablespoons of the stock in a large saucepan. Add the onion, leeks, potatoes and nuts and stir-fry in the stock over a medium heat for 5 minutes. Bring to the boil and add the rest of the stock. Cover and simmer until the potatoes are cooked but still intact (about 25 minutes). Allow to cool slightly, then liquidize. Return to the saucepan and reheat gently with the herbs and seasoning. Do not boil.

Watercress Soup

Watercress gives a pungent taste to this satisfying soup.

1½ pints (900ml) vegetable stock
1 large onion, finely chopped
1 clove garlic, crushed
1lb (450g) potatoes, scrubbed and cubed
large pinch mixed dried herbs
sea salt and freshly ground black pepper
1 bunch watercress, washed and chopped

Preparation time: 10 minutes
Cooking time: 35 minutes

Heat 3–4 tablespoons of the vegetable stock in a large saucepan then add the onion, garlic and potatoes. Cook on a medium heat for 5 minutes, then bring to the boil. Add the herbs, salt and pepper, and cook until the potatoes are tender – about 20 minutes. Add the watercress and cook for a further 5 minutes. Cool slightly, then liquidize. Return to the saucepan and reheat gently, stirring in more stock or water if the soup is too thick.

Carrot Soup

Another 'main meal' soup, colourful, filling and tasty.

1 large onion, chopped
1 clove garlic, crushed
1 sprig fresh rosemary, chopped, or ½ teaspoon dried
rosemary
1lb (450g) carrots, finely chopped
1½ pints (900ml) vegetable stock
½ teaspoon mild curry powder
1 tablespoon medium oatmeal
sea salt

Preparation time: 5 minutes
Cooking time: 30 minutes

Cook the onion, garlic, rosemary and carrots in 2–3 table-spoons stock over a medium heat for about 5 minutes, then bring to the boil. Add the rest of the stock, the curry powder, oatmeal and salt, then cover the saucepan, lower the heat, and simmer for about 20 minutes or until the carrots are soft. Blend in a liquidizer then return to the saucepan, reheating gently. Add more stock or water if the soup is too thick.

Brussels Sprout Soup with Yoghurt

If you like Brussels sprouts, you'll love this soup.

1½ pints (900ml) vegetable stock
1lb (450g) Brussels sprouts, trimmed and finely chopped
1 large onion, finely chopped
sea salt and freshly ground black pepper
2 strips lemon rind
2 teaspoons soya flour
1 carton low-fat natural live yoghurt or plain soya yoghurt
3 tablespoons chopped fresh parsley

Preparation time: 10 minutes
Cooking time: 35 minutes

Heat 2–3 tablespoons of the stock in a large saucepan and sweat the sprouts and onions over a medium heat, stirring all the time, for 10 minutes. Add the remaining stock and bring to the boil. Lower the heat, season, add the lemon rind, then cover and simmer for about 20 minutes. Remove the lemon rind, liquidize the soup then return to the saucepan. Mix the soya flour with the yoghurt then stir into the soup with the parsley. Do not allow to boil, or the yoghurt may curdle.

Jerusalem Artichoke Soup

Jerusalem artichokes are knobbly and offputting in appearance, but make delightful soups. Here is a very simple recipe.

1 pint (600ml) vegetable stock
2–3 large leeks, washed and chopped
1lb (450g) artichokes, scrubbed or peeled, and chopped
2 medium carrots, diced
1 bay leaf
1 teaspoon fresh or ½ teaspoon dried basil
1 clove garlic, crushed
sea salt and freshly ground black pepper

Preparation time: 10 minutes
Cooking time: 25 minutes

Put the stock in a saucepan with the vegetables and bring to the boil. Add the herbs, garlic and seasoning, lower the heat and simmer for about 20 minutes, or until the artichokes are cooked. Liquidize, then return to the saucepan and reheat gently. Do not boil as this impairs the flavour.

Spinach and Tofu Soup

A light and creamy soup which requires minimal cooking time.

2¼ pints (1.35l) vegetable stock
2 packs Tofeata or Morinaga tofu, drained and
cut into cubes
2lb (900g) spinach, washed and roughly chopped
sea salt and freshly ground black pepper
chopped fresh parsley to garnish

Preparation time: 5 minutes
Cooking time: 20 minutes

Bring the stock to the boil in a pan. Add the tofu and spinach and bring back to the boil, then cover and simmer for 10 minutes, stirring occasionally. Liquidize if liked, when cooled slightly. Add salt and pepper and reheat. Sprinkle over the chopped parsley just before serving.

Green Split Pea Soup

Versatile split peas, available very cheaply from any supermarket, can easily be made into appetizing soups.

12oz (350g) dried green split peas
½ green pepper, chopped
1½ pints (900ml) vegetable stock
1 stick celery, finely chopped
1 medium onion, chopped
1 carrot, finely chopped or grated
½ teaspoon fresh or ¼ teaspoon dried marjoram
sea salt and freshly ground black pepper

Preparation time: 10–15 minutes
Cooking time: about 2¼ hours (but you don't have to stand over it all the time)

In a large saucepan, bring the split peas and green pepper to the boil in the stock. Lower the heat and simmer very gently for about 1¼ hours. Add the remaining ingredients and simmer for another 45 minutes, or until everything is tender. Liquidize if liked, after cooling slightly, then reheat and check the seasoning.

CHAPTER NINE

STARTERS AND DIPS

Although classed as starters, many of these dishes make complete light meals in themselves. They are particularly suitable for lunches, for when you are on your own, or when you haven't much time to prepare a full-scale meal. Although they are all anti-cellulite not all these dishes are low-calorie.

When recipes specify olive oil make sure you always use one labelled 'extra-virgin'. It is slightly more expensive but it really is worth it. Although olive oil is the best sort of oil to use, as it is monounsaturated, it does have rather a strong taste and if you don't like it you can substitute a cold-pressed sesame or grapeseed oil, which have hardly any taste at all.

Hummous

There are many versions of hummous, a Greek dish based on chick peas. Over the years I must have tried them all, and this one is my favourite.

1 14oz (400g) tin chick peas, drained and rinsed (or you can cook your own according to the instructions on page 118)

1 dessertspoon tahini
juice 1 lemon
1 clove garlic, crushed
2 tablespoons olive oil
1 tablespoon low-fat natural yoghurt
1 dessertspoon chopped fresh parsley
sea salt and freshly ground black pepper
paprika to garnish

Preparation time: about 5 minutes
Cooking time: nil

This must be one of the easiest dishes ever devised, if you have a liquidizer. If not, I should imagine it's murder. Simply put all the ingredients except the paprika into the liquidizer and blend on top speed until a smooth paste is formed. Turn into a suitable dish and garnish with paprika.

Serve with crudités – sticks of carrot and celery, chunks of broccoli or cauliflower, and green and red peppers. You can also serve hummous with manna or gluten-free bread, or spread on oatcakes or barleycakes. You will not need to spread butter or margarine on first.

Avocado Dip

Avocados are high in fat, but they do not encourage cellulite to form. This dip is good with crudités, or it can be spread on manna bread or oatcakes, like the hummous.

1 large ripe avocado
1 pack tofu
juice of 1 lemon, or to taste
2 tablespoons cold-pressed sunflower or grapeseed oil
sea salt and freshly ground black pepper

Preparation time: about 5 minutes
Cooking time: nil

Peel and stone the avocado and chop into small pieces. Break up the tofu in a bowl. Put all the ingredients in a blender and blend until smooth. Serve with raw carrots, broccoli, etc, as for hummous.

Sunflower Dip

4oz (125g) sunflower seeds, ground
1 clove garlic, crushed
1 stick celery, very finely chopped
juice ½ lemon

Preparation time: 5 minutes
Cooking time: nil

Blend all the ingredients in a liquidizer on high speed. Add spring water to make this dip more runny if necessary.

Cashew and Tofu Pâté

This is a more 'festive', sophisticated pâté, for special occasions or dinner parties.

2 tablespoons vegetable stock
1 small onion or shallot, very finely chopped
1 clove garlic, crushed
1 pack Morinaga or Tofeata tofu
4oz (125g) ground cashew nuts
1 tablespoon olive oil
4 tablespoons spring or filtered water (or, for a very special
occasion, you could use white wine)
2 tablespoons chopped fresh parsley, or (in an emergency)
2 teaspoons dried
sea salt and freshly ground black pepper

Preparation time: about 10 minutes
Cooking time: 5 minutes

Heat the vegetable stock in a saucepan and gently stir-fry the onion and garlic over a medium heat until softened. Remove from the heat. In a large mixing bowl, mash the tofu with a fork, then add the onion and garlic. Now add the nuts, olive oil, water or wine, parsley, salt and pepper and stir well. Press the pâté into 1 large or 4 small earthenware dishes and chill in the fridge for an hour or two, if possible, before serving.

Quark and Walnut Dip

Although the emphasis of this book is on non-dairy foods, quark – the low-fat cheese made with skimmed milk – does no harm occasionally. This dip tastes much creamier and more calorific than it actually is. The onions are essential.

8oz (225g) quark
1 tablespoon olive oil
sea salt and freshly ground black pepper
1 small onion, very finely chopped, or 1 teaspoon
onion granules
1 tablespoon chopped fresh parsley
2oz (50g) walnuts, ground

Preparation time: 10 minutes
Cooking time: nil

Put all the ingredients into a liquidizer and blend on high speed until completely homogenized. If the dip is too thick, add a little spring water or skimmed milk and blend again.

Aubergine and Tahini Dip

Although aubergines taste wonderful in dips, they are rather a nuisance to prepare, as they take ages. However, once in a while it is worth taking the trouble to make this delicious dip.

1 large or 2 small aubergines
2 tablespoons tahini
juice 1 lemon
1 clove garlic, crushed
2 tablespoons finely chopped fresh parsley
sea salt and freshly ground black pepper

Preparation time: 10 minutes
Cooking time: 1 hour

Preheat the oven to 350°F, 180°C, gas mark 4. Bake the aubergine for about 1 hour, or until soft – test with a fork. Hold the aubergine under the cold tap and peel off the purple skin. Then put all the ingredients into a liquidizer and blend on high speed. Transfer to a glass or earthenware container and chill for an hour or two, if possible, although the dip can be eaten straight away if required.

Vegetable Pâté

This pâté can be eaten by itself, with a salad, used as a dip or as a spread on oatmeal biscuits.

1 stick celery, chopped
½ cucumber, chopped
1 medium green pepper, chopped
1 medium onion, finely chopped
½ teaspoon fresh or dried dill weed
4oz (125g) cottage cheese or quark
sea salt and freshly ground black pepper

Preparation time: 5 minutes
Cooking time: nil

Place all the ingredients in a liquidizer and blend on high speed until a smooth paste is formed – it won't be completely smooth, though.

Asparagus with Yoghurt Dressing

This is a healthy version of the more usual asparagus with melted butter or hollandaise sauce.

1 small onion, finely chopped, or ½ teaspoon onion powder
½ clove garlic, crushed
juice ½ lemon
1 carton low-fat live yoghurt
1 large bunch asparagus

Preparation time: 5 minutes
Cooking time: about 10 minutes

First, make the yoghurt dressing by mixing together the onion, garlic, lemon juice and yoghurt. Then trim the asparagus and boil in salted water until tender – about 10 minutes. Drain, and serve warm with the yoghurt dressing.

Quick and Easy Burgers

These burgers do not need cooking and, with a salad, make a complete meal in themselves.

4oz (125g) cashews, almonds or mixed nuts, ground
8oz (225g) quark or cottage cheese
3 tablespoons chopped fresh parsley
1 small onion, grated or finely chopped – or use ½ teaspoon
onion granules
sea salt and freshly ground black pepper
wholemeal breadcrumbs for coating

Preparation time: about 5 minutes
Cooking time: nil

In a large mixing bowl combine the ground nuts, quark or cottage cheese, parsley, onion and seasoning. The mixture will be fairly stiff. Divide into 4 and form into burger shapes. Roll in breadcrumbs and put in the fridge until required.

Raita

This version of the well-known cool accompaniment to hot Indian dishes is also good as a dip in its own right.

½ cucumber, finely chopped
sea salt and freshly ground black pepper
1 teaspoon caraway seeds
1 tablespoon fresh mint, chopped
2–3 spring onions, finely chopped
1 carton low-fat live yoghurt

Preparation time: 5 minutes
Cooking time: nil
Mix all the ingredients together well and serve immediately.

Mushrooms à la Grecque

A sophisticated starter – but you've got to like garlic.

¼ pint (150ml) water
2 cloves garlic, crushed
juice 2 lemons
2 tablespoons olive oil
1 bay leaf
sea salt and freshly ground black pepper
12oz (350g) button mushrooms
1 firm tomato, skinned and chopped
2 tablespoons chopped fresh parsley

Preparation time: 10 minutes
Cooking time: 10 minutes

Put all the ingredients except the parsley, mushrooms and tomato into a saucepan, bring to the boil and boil for 5 minutes. Add the mushrooms, lower the heat and simmer for another 5 minutes. Remove from the heat and add the chopped tomato. Sprinkle with the parsley. Allow to cool, then refrigerate for an hour or two before serving.

Stuffed Tomatoes

Shirley Conran is famous for saying that life is too short to stuff a mushroom. But it's not too short to stuff a tomato, and this delicious recipe takes hardly any time at all. Tomatoes can also be stuffed with rice salad (see pages 88–9).

4 large, firm tomatoes (don't choose really huge ones, but they must be firm)
4oz (125g) wholemeal breadcrumbs
4oz (125g) quark, cottage or other low-fat soft cheese, such as fromage frais
2 tablespoons finely chopped chives
sea salt and freshly ground black pepper
parsley to garnish

Preparation time: 7–8 minutes
Cooking time: nil

Cut a lid off the top of the tomatoes and carefully scoop out the flesh, making sure you don't cut the outside of the tomatoes. Chop the pulp and transfer to a mixing bowl. Add all the remaining ingredients except the parsley and mix well. Fill the tomatoes with the mixture, garnish with parsley, and replace the lids. Serve chilled.

CHAPTER TEN

SALADS AND DRESSINGS

Salads are, of course, the mainstay of the anti-cellulite diet. Even if you haven't always got the time or the ingredients for a full-scale salad, you should make sure you have something raw at every meal, as to some extent this will work to detoxify any less healthy food you might have eaten or be about to eat.

However, in the anti-cellulite diet salads are the stars, rather than being relegated to bit-players. The whole concept of what constitutes a salad has undergone a dramatic change in recent years, and these days they can be complete and satisfying meals in themselves.

When possible, make sure the salad ingredients are really fresh and organically grown. Organic produce tastes quite different from the other kind, even if its appearance may not be quite so attractive.

It is important that salads should be colourful, as this makes them look more appetizing. Fortunately this is easy, as the raw ingredients tend to be colourful in their own right. Always make sure your salad has a variety of colours.

Do get into the habit of buying fresh sprouted grains, such as beansprouts, alfalfa or others, now available from most supermarkets. You can even sprout your own, and many vegetarian cookery books have instructions for doing this. I have found that the bought sprouts are just as good as the ones you attempt yourself. Sprouted grains can be strewn over the top of just about any salad – you don't need special recipes on how to use them. However, they don't last very long and should be eaten either on the day of purchase or the next day.

Sprouted grains contain many important nutrients, and all have a slight pea/beany taste, so they won't seem as unfamiliar as all that. Otherwise, look carefully at the salad section in your supermarket or greengrocer's. You will find that there is far more available these days than limp lettuce, tomatoes and cucumber. There are now many different types of salad greens around, and these all add interest and taste to a salad.

Once you have got into the habit of eating a salad at every meal you will soon find that you miss it if it is not there. Salad ingredients are not expensive, and even the most pricy lettuce or exotic vegetables will be far cheaper than junk foods and processed meats.

Here are some ideas for salads, and also for unusual dressings to accompany them. There is no need to peel the vegetables unless specifically instructed to do so by the recipe. Do avoid bought mayonnaise and salad dressings; they contain huge amounts of fat, and probably artificial preservatives as well.

Preparation times are not given in this section, as the salads take only minutes to prepare.

Nut and Rice Salad

8oz (225g) brown rice, cooked
4oz (125g) red cabbage, grated
1 green pepper, finely chopped
1 carrot, grated
1oz (25g) chopped nuts – hazels, almonds or cashews
1oz (25g) sultanas

Mix all the ingredients together and serve with one of the dressings on pages 96–101.

Kidney Bean and Rice Salad

This is an extremely healthy and filling salad, containing lots of soluble fibre in the form of fresh vegetables and brown rice, all mixed together in a harmonious whole.

1 tin red kidney beans, drained – any size will do
4oz (125g) cooked brown rice
½ iceberg lettuce, washed and sliced or torn into strips
2 sticks celery, very finely chopped
½ cucumber, washed and very finely chopped
vinaigrette (see page 96)

Combine all the ingredients together, mixing well and adding just enough vinaigrette to coat the ingredients, but not so there is dressing swimming at the bottom.
Note: you could use other pulses for this salad, such as chick

peas or butter beans, but kidney beans are the most flavourful, as well as the most colourful. You can spoon this salad into hot pitta bread if you like.

Walnut Salad with Figs

A very satisfying salad, and it's even nicer with fresh figs than with dried.

½ small white cabbage, grated
4 carrots, grated
1 onion, very finely chopped
1 cooking apple, grated
yoghurt or tofu dressing (see pages 98, 101)
4oz (125g) fresh or dried figs, sliced
2 dessert apples, finely sliced
juice 1 orange
4oz (125g) walnut pieces

Mix together the cabbage, carrots, onion and cooking apple. Stir in the dressing, mix well together, then arrange the slices of figs and dessert apples on top. Pour over the orange juice then scatter the walnuts over the salad.

Waldorf Salad

This salad is a universal favourite.

2 large dessert apples, cored and sliced
2 sticks celery, washed and sliced
2oz (50g) walnuts
2oz (50g) hazelnuts
2oz (50g) sultanas
chopped fresh parsley
yoghurt dressing (see page 101)

Mix the apples, celery, nuts, sultanas and parsley together
and combine with the yoghurt dressing.

Date Salad

A wonderfully colourful and tasty salad which will cheer you
up if you need cheering up.

½ iceberg lettuce, washed and sliced or torn into strips
4 oranges, peeled and thinly sliced
4oz (125g) dates, stoned and finely chopped. Use fresh ones
if possible – they are getting more widely available all the time
2oz (50g) flaked almonds
lemon dressing (see page 97)

Put the lettuce in a serving bowl and arrange the orange
slices, dates and almonds on top. Pour the lemon dressing
over, but not so much that it swims at the bottom.

New Potato Salad

An exciting way to use new potatoes when they first come into season.

1lb (450g) new potatoes
2 tablespoons chopped fresh mint
tofu dressing (see page 98)

Cook the potatoes in boiling salted water until tender, then rinse under the tap in a colander to cool. Cut into small pieces and mix in a bowl with the mint and the tofu dressing. Keep in the fridge until required, then serve with a green salad.

Carrot Salad with Apples

juice ½ lemon
3 dessert apples, cored and sliced
1lb (450g) carrots, grated
3 tablespoons raisins
1 tablespoon sunflower seeds
2 tablespoons broken cashew nuts
½ iceberg lettuce, washed and sliced or torn into strips
vinaigrette (see page 96)

Sprinkle the lemon juice over the apples to prevent discoloration then mix with the carrots, raisins, sunflower seeds and nuts. Put the lettuce in a bowl, add the carrot, nut and apple mixture, then toss in the vinaigrette dressing.

Mixed Salad

Green salads can consist of just lettuce, cucumber and green peppers. This salad is slightly more special.

½ iceberg lettuce, washed and sliced or torn into strips
1 bunch watercress, washed and chopped
2–3 spring onions, finely chopped
2 courgettes, grated
2 carrots, grated
4 tomatoes, sliced
sunflower or pumpkin seeds
sunflower, vinaigrette, tofu or tahini dressing
(see pages 96, 98, 99)

Combine all the salad ingredients and toss in the vinaigrette, tofu or tahini dressing.

Experiment with other green leaves in salads – the choice has never been wider. Choose from lamb's lettuce, cos lettuce, Chinese leaves, radicchio – a strong, red lettuce which has made its appearance in British supermarkets recently – chicory, spinach leaves (use raw), nasturtium leaves, celery leaves, dandelion leaves (as long as they are young and very green). It is a good idea to keep a wooden bowl specially for green salads. Rub a clove of garlic round the inside first, and then just wipe after using. It should not need washing up.

Other vegetables can easily be added to a green salad – raw cauliflower or broccoli florets, or avocado slices, for example. Nuts, such as walnuts or hazelnuts, can also be added.

Greek Salad

You can now buy low-fat vegetarian feta cheese, which makes this popular Greek salad suitable for cellulite-shifters. Don't buy the high-fat, animal-rennet variety.

1 pack vegetarian feta cheese
½ iceberg lettuce, washed and sliced or torn into strips
½ cucumber, cut into chunks
4–5 firm tomatoes, cut into chunks
12 black olives
vinaigrette dressing (see page 96)

In a glass bowl, combine all the salad ingredients and toss in the vinaigrette dressing.

Pine Nut Salad

Once a rare delicacy, pine nuts are now easily available, and have a rich, rather slippery, taste when fresh.

4 tomatoes, chopped
6 radishes, finely chopped
½ iceberg lettuce, washed and sliced or torn into strips
3 tablespoons finely chopped fresh parsley
1 packet alfalfa sprouts
3oz (75g) pine nuts
vinaigrette or yoghurt dressing (see pages 96, 101)

Mix all the salad ingredients together and toss in vinaigrette or yoghurt dressing.

Leek and Hazelnut Salad

Leeks are one of my favourite vegetables. They need a very little cooking for this salad, but not much, and certainly not enough to affect the vitamin content.

> 2 large leeks, washed and sliced in rings
> 1 red pepper, seeded and sliced
> 2oz (50g) hazelnuts, chopped
> sea salt and freshly ground black pepper
> vinaigrette or yoghurt dressing (see pages 96, 101)

Blanch the leeks in boiling salted water for 2 minutes, then cool by rinsing under the cold tap in a colander. Arrange the leeks, pepper and hazelnuts in a glass bowl, season, and toss in vinaigrette or yoghurt dressing.

Coleslaw

There are many ways of making coleslaw, but this one is tasty as well as healthy.

> ½ white cabbage, grated or finely sliced
> 2 large carrots, grated
> ½ teaspoon caraway seeds
> freshly ground black pepper
> yoghurt or tofu dressing (see pages 98, 101)

Combine all the ingredients, including the dressing, in a bowl. This coleslaw will keep for up to 4 days in the fridge, if kept covered.

Cauliflower Salad

Cauliflower can be eaten raw – as crudités, for example – but if preferred, can be steamed for about 5 minutes first for this salad. The dates give a 'comforting' feel to this vegetable and fruit combination.

1 small or ½ large cauliflower, cut into small florets
2oz (50g) dates, either dried or fresh
2 bananas, sliced
1 packet alfalfa sprouts
tofu, yoghurt or tahini dressing (see pages 98, 99, 101) or
soya mayonnaise (see page 100)

If steaming the cauliflower first, cook for 5 minutes then cool quickly by rinsing in a colander under the cold tap. Combine all the salad ingredients in a mixing bowl then add the dressing of your choice (they all go well).

Raw Beetroot Salad

8oz (225g) raw beetroot, peeled and grated
2 sticks celery, very finely chopped
2 large dessert apples, cored and chopped
vinaigrette or tahini dressing (see pages 96, 99)

Combine the beetroot, celery and apples then mix in the dressing – just enough to moisten the salad.

Spinach and Cauliflower Salad

This salad uses raw cauliflower, so make sure all the florets are very crisp and crunchy, and don't leave in any woody cauliflower stems.

8oz (225g) new potatoes, cooked with mint, then cooled
1 medium cauliflower, cut into very small florets
1lb (450g) spinach, washed and torn into strips
2–3 dessert apples, cored and sliced
2oz (50g) sunflower or soya cheese, cubed or sliced
vinaigrette dressing (see below)

If the potatoes are very tiny, leave whole. Otherwise, slice them and mix with the remaining salad ingredients. Toss in the vinaigrette.

DRESSINGS

Vinaigrette Dressing

It is a good idea to make up this dressing in advance and then keep it in a screwtop jar in the fridge until required. It keeps well, and is suitable for most salads.

6 fl oz (175ml) cold-pressed olive oil, or other
cold-pressed oil
3 fl oz (75ml) white wine vinegar

½ teaspoon honey
½ teaspoon sea salt
½ teaspoon freshly ground black pepper
1 teaspoon fresh or ½ teaspoon dried tarragon
½ teaspoon made mustard

Put all the ingredients in a bottle with a screwtop lid and shake thoroughly. This dressing is best left a day or two before use for the flavours to meld together. Before using, shake thoroughly again.

Lemon Dressing

juice 1 lemon
twice as much cold-pressed olive, safflower or sunflower
seed oil as lemon juice
a little sea salt and freshly ground black pepper

Mix all the ingredients together. This dressing is good if you are just starting an anti-cellulite regime. You can even just squeeze the juice of a lemon on a salad if you like.

Avocado and Cashew Dressing

4oz (125g) cashew nuts, ground
½ avocado
juice ½ lemon
sea salt and freshly ground black pepper
½ onion, very finely chopped or grated
¼ pint (150ml) water

Blend all the ingredients in a liquidizer. Add only a very small amount of water at first, then keep adding as required, while the liquidizer is on high speed, until the desired consistency is reached. This dressing is very rich, and a little goes a long way.

Sunflower Seed Dressing

A lighter dressing which goes very well with green salads.

4oz (125g) sunflower seeds, ground
1 clove garlic, crushed
1 stick celery, very finely chopped
juice ½ lemon
water

Blend all the ingredients in a liquidizer, adding water slowly until the required consistency is obtained.

Tofu Dressing

This dressing looks exactly like mayonnaise, and can be used in all salad recipes where mayonnaise is specified.

1 pack tofu, drained
1 tablespoon cold-pressed olive oil
1 teaspoon lemon juice

1 tablespoon very finely chopped onion, or use
onion powder
1 teaspoon honey
sea salt and freshly ground black pepper to taste

Put all the ingredients in a liquidizer and blend until smooth.

Tahini Dressing

Tahini, available from healthfood shops, is sesame seed paste
and is very useful in an anti-cellulite diet. Over the years it
has become indispensable to me and I've grown to love it. It
tastes something like peanut butter but has more of an edge
to it.

¼ pint (150ml) tahini
1 carton natural low-fat or soya yoghurt
juice 1 lemon
1 clove garlic, crushed, or use onion powder
2–3 tablespoons chopped fresh parsley
¼ teaspoon cayenne pepper
sea salt to taste

Liquidize all the ingredients together on high speed until
smooth. This dressing will keep for up to three days in the
fridge.

Cashew Dressing

4oz (125g) cashew nuts, ground
1 cup filtered water
2 cloves garlic, crushed, or use onion powder
juice 1 lemon
1 teaspoon Vecon

Blend all the ingredients together in a liquidizer on high speed. This dressing is a good substitute for mayonnaise.

Soya Mayonnaise

Beware with this one – it's *horribly* delicious. I first came across it in The Country Life restaurant in Heddon Street, London W1, which is run by the vegan Seventh-Day Adventists. The only way I can stop myself pigging on this mayonnaise is to make only very minute quantities. However, for four people you will need:

1 carton soya milk
1 teaspoon sea salt
1 teaspoon onion powder or finely chopped onion
8 fl oz (250ml) olive oil
2 tablespoons lemon juice
1–2 tablespoons chopped fresh parsley, or use oregano,
basil or thyme

Blend the soya milk, salt and onion on high speed. As the blender is whirring round, pour in the olive oil very slowly.

The more oil you pour, the thicker the mayonnaise will become. Transfer to a mixing bowl and fold the lemon juice and herbs into the mixture. This can be used like ordinary mayonnaise on salads, in jacket potatoes, or as a spread on wholemeal bread. It keeps for three or four days in a screwtop jar in the fridge.

Yoghurt Dressing

1 carton low-fat yoghurt
1 onion, finely chopped, or 1 teaspoon onion granules
½ clove garlic, crushed
juice ½ lemon
sea salt and freshly ground black pepper

Mix all the ingredients together or blend in a liquidizer.

Simple Avocado Dressing

½ large avocado, or 1 whole small one, peeled and stoned
juice ½ lemon
1 clove garlic, crushed
¼ teaspoon onion powder
sea salt and freshly ground black pepper

Blend all the ingredients together in a liquidizer. If the mixture is too stiff, add water rather than more lemon juice.

CHAPTER ELEVEN

VEGETARIAN MAIN COURSES

JACKET POTATOES

These are the easiest vegetables to start you off on an anti-cellulite cookery regime. Try to buy organically grown potatoes if possible – as with other vegetables, this is getting easier all the time.

Cooking potatoes in their jackets conserves all their goodness – especially as most of the nutrients are found in or near the skin – and it is simplicity itself. Just preheat the oven to 400°F, 200°C, or gas mark 6, scrub the potatoes, prick with a fork and cook at the top of the oven for about an hour. Do not rub with butter or cover in aluminium foil (which is now being associated with the degeneration of tissues). If you use a microwave, jacket potatoes will take about 10 minutes to cook, according to size.

Cellulite-shifters should eat their potatoes with a salad, or one of the dips in the chapter on Starters and Dips. The rest of the family can add all the butter and cheese they like. Jacket potatoes can accompany any dish at all, and are a wonderful standby. They also leave everybody feeling pleasantly full, and I have yet to come across somebody who doesn't like them.

Cellulite-shifters should not ever eat chips or mash their potatoes with cream, milk or butter. You can mash them with a little low-fat yoghurt if you like, but that's all.

CURRIES

Curries are extremely easy to prepare and have the advantage of making ordinary vegetables tastier and more special. Many vegetables become easier to eat when delicately spiced, but don't overdo the spices in the belief that the more you add, the more exotic the dish will taste. The idea is to complement the natural taste of the vegetables. Once you've cooked a few of the curries suggested below, you will soon notice a difference between the home-cooked variety and those traditionally served in Indian restaurants, which tend to be oily and highly salted. *Always* use brown rice. It takes a little longer to cook than white, although many of the newer types of brown rice on sale are 'quick-cook', but the difference in taste is worth it. Once you are used to brown rice you will never want to go back to the white variety again.

Carrot and Mushroom Curry

This curry is delicately spiced and the spices complement, rather than overpower, the taste of the vegetables.

8oz (225g) brown rice
4 cups water (double the quantity of rice)
1 level teaspoon sea salt, or to taste

½ pint (300ml) vegetable stock, either homemade or made
with Vecon or other vegetable concentrate
1 teaspoon grated or finely chopped fresh ginger root, or
½ teaspoon powdered ginger
1 teaspoon ground turmeric
1 teaspoon ground cumin
1 teaspoon ground coriander
2 medium onions, finely chopped
2 large tomatoes, skinned
4 large carrots, finely chopped
8oz (225g) mushrooms, chopped – use large, flat, open
mushrooms, if possible
1 teaspoon garam masala
sea salt to taste
2 tablespoons chopped coriander leaves to garnish
(optional – but recommended)

Preparation time: about 15 minutes
Cooking time: 25–30 minutes altogether, depending on type
of brown rice used. Holland and Barrett sell excellent quick-
cooking brown rice.

Put the rice, cold water and sea salt in a pan and bring to the
boil, lower the heat and simmer until tender. Meanwhile
prepare the vegetables: pour half the stock into a large
saucepan on a medium heat. Add the ginger, turmeric,
cumin, coriander and onions, stirring all the time. Cook for
about 10 minutes, then add the rest of the stock and the
tomatoes, carrots and mushrooms. Bring to the boil, then
lower the heat and simmer for about 25 minutes or until the

vegetables are cooked. Stir in the garam masala, add salt and continue to cook for another minute. Stir in the coriander leaves if used and serve straight away with the rice.

This curry should be served with a salad. Low-fat yoghurt or raita (see page 83) can also be served as an accompaniment.

Broccoli, Sesame Seed and Brown Rice Curry

A quick, easy and tasty favourite.

½ pint (300ml) vegetable stock, made with Vecon or
vegetable stock cube
1lb (450g) broccoli, chopped
8oz (225g) mushrooms, washed and chopped
2 tablespoons sesame seeds
sea salt and freshly ground black pepper
1 level teaspoon mild curry powder or garam masala
8oz (225g) brown rice, cooked

Preparation time: about 10 minutes
Cooking time: about 20 minutes

Heat about ¼ pint (150ml) of the stock in a saucepan and add the broccoli. Stir-fry for 3 minutes, then add the chopped mushrooms and stir for another 2 minutes. Add the remaining stock, bring to the boil then cover and simmer until the broccoli is just tender – about 10 minutes. Add the sesame seeds, salt and pepper and stir for 1 minute. Add the rice and curry powder and stir until thoroughly heated through. Serve at once with a mixed salad.

Note: the rice for this dish is even nicer if cooked in vegetable stock rather than plain water.

Spinach Curry

As you proceed with the anti-cellulite regime you will probably find yourself buying lots and lots of spinach. Fresh is best, of course, but frozen leaf spinach comes a very close second. Don't forget that spinach goes down alarmingly when being cooked, so always buy at least twice as much as you imagine you will need.

8oz (225g) brown rice
2lb (900g) spinach, washed and roughly chopped
½ pint (300ml) vegetable stock
1 large onion, finely chopped
2–3 green peppers, seeded and sliced
1 clove garlic, crushed or finely chopped
2 teaspoons ground coriander
2 teaspoons ground cumin
¼ teaspoon cayenne pepper
sea salt
1 tablespoon tomato purée, or 2–3 fresh tomatoes,
skinned and chopped

Preparation time: 10–15 minutes
Cooking time: 25–30 minutes

Put the rice on to cook according to the instructions on the packet. Add a little salt. When the rice has come to the boil, start preparing the curry. First cook the spinach by putting it in a saucepan without any extra water – plenty will emerge as it cooks. Bring to the boil, cook for about 10 minutes, then remove from the heat and drain by pressing it hard to make it as dry as possible. Chop very finely on a board. Heat vegetable stock in a saucepan and add the onion, peppers, garlic, spices and salt. Cook on a medium heat until the onion and peppers are soft – about 10 minutes. Stir in the spinach and tomato purée or fresh chopped tomatoes, and continue to cook for another 2 minutes. Serve at once with the rice.

Root Vegetable Curry

This is a very tasty and filling dish for winter, and will satisfy the hungriest eater.

8oz (225g) brown rice
1½ pints (990ml) vegetable stock
8oz (225g) turnips, peeled and cubed
8oz (225g) potatoes, peeled and cubed
8oz (225g) carrots, sliced
1 teaspoon ground turmeric
1 teaspoon ground cumin
1 teaspoon ground coriander
1 teaspoon garam masala
½ teaspoon cayenne pepper
2 bay leaves
2 cloves garlic, crushed or finely chopped
approx ½ teaspoon sea salt
2 tablespoons chopped coriander leaves (optional)

Preparation time: 25–30 minutes
Cooking time: 40 minutes

Put the rice on to cook according to the instructions on the packet. When it is simmering, start the curry. Heat about ¼ pint (150ml) of the vegetable stock in a large saucepan and add the vegetables and spices. Stir over a medium heat for about 5 minutes, then bring to the boil. Add the rest of the stock, the bay leaves, garlic and salt. Lower the heat, cover and simmer for about 20 minutes or until the potatoes are done. Add the coriander, if using, then serve with the rice.

Cauliflower Curry

Cauliflowers lend themselves extremely well to curries and this one is colourful as well as tasty.

8oz (225g) brown rice
½ pint (300ml) vegetable stock
1 clove garlic, crushed
1 teaspoon ground cumin
1 teaspoon ground coriander
1 teaspoon grated fresh ginger root, or ½ teaspoon
powdered ginger
1 teaspoon ground turmeric
sea salt to taste
1 large onion, finely chopped
1 cauliflower, cut into small florets. Discard any
tough-looking stalks
1 tablespoon tomato purée
4 large tomatoes, skinned and sliced

Preparation time: 10 minutes
Cooking time: about 30 minutes

Put the rice on to cook according to the instructions on the packet. When it has been simmering for 5 minutes, begin the curry. Heat half the vegetable stock in a large saucepan and add the garlic, spices, salt, onion and cauliflower. Stir over a medium heat for 5 minutes, then add the remaining stock and the tomato purée. Bring to the boil, then lower the heat, cover and simmer for 15 minutes. Just before serving, add the skinned and sliced tomatoes and serve at once with the rice.

CHINESE-STYLE DISHES

Chinese cookery lends itself very easily to the anti-cellulite regime, so long as you always stir-fry in stock rather than in any kind of oil. The secret of successful Chinese cookery is to chop up the vegetables very finely and prepare the sauce beforehand, as this is a very quick method of cooking and you need to have all the ingredients to hand. Don't worry if you haven't got a wok; a large non-stick frying pan or saucepan will do. Although this method of cookery is very quick and easy, it does need constant attention.

Chinese-style anti-cellulite cookery has a sophisticated taste and is more suitable for adults than children. I discovered it when I was trying to work out interesting dishes to keep me on my anti-cellulite diet, and found it a real taste sensation – so much cleaner and fresher-tasting than the kind of Chinese dishes, heavily reliant on oil and monosodium glutamate, that one finds in some Chinese restaurants.

Broccoli with Bamboo Shoots and Water Chestnuts

FOR THE RICE:
8oz (225g) brown rice
4 cups water (or twice as much as the rice)
1 teaspoon sea salt

FOR THE SAUCE:
1 tablespoon vegetable stock
1 teaspoon cornflour
2 tablespoons dry sherry
1 tablespoon low-salt soy sauce

½ cup vegetable stock
8oz (225g) broccoli, finely chopped
2 tablespoons bean sprouts
1 clove garlic, crushed
1 teaspoon grated fresh ginger
1 small tin water chestnuts, finely sliced
1 small tin bamboo shoots

Preparation time: 10 minutes at most
Cooking time: 25–35 minutes, depending on rice

Put the rice and water in a saucepan, add salt and bring to the boil. Then cover and simmer (do not stir) for about 25 minutes. Once the rice is simmering, make sure all the vegetables are ready, then make the sauce by mixing all the ingredients together in a bowl. Set aside.

Heat the stock in a large non-stick saucepan and stir-fry the broccoli, bean sprouts, garlic and ginger for 3 minutes. Lower the heat to medium and add the water chestnuts and bamboo shoots. Stir-fry for 2 minutes then add the sauce. Turn down the heat and simmer for 2 minutes. Serve immediately with the rice.

Braised Vegetables with Chinese Noodles

This is a highly sophisticated dish, suitable for dinner parties. It is especially suitable for anybody who is on a low-salt, low-fat or low-carbohydrate diet for any reason – good for slimmers and those who have to watch their food intake for health reasons.

FOR THE SAUCE
2 tablespoons dry sherry
1 tablespoon soy sauce
1 tablespoon vegetable stock
1 teaspoon cornflour

8oz (225g) noodles – if using the Chinese noodles in
compressed squares, allow 1 square per person
8 fl oz (250ml) vegetable stock
4oz (125g) mangetout peas, stems and strings removed
8oz (225g) Chinese or white cabbage, shredded

8oz (225g) mushrooms, finely chopped
2 medium carrots, finely chopped
2 shallots or small onions, finely chopped
1 small green pepper, seeded and sliced
1 small red pepper, seeded and sliced
4oz (125g) beansprouts
1 tablespoon sesame seeds, roasted. (You can dry-roast
sesame seeds by stirring them for 1–2 minutes in a pan on a
high heat. Keep stirring, or they will stick and burn.)

Preparation time: 15 minutes
Cooking time: 10 minutes

First, make the sauce by mixing together all the ingredients
in a bowl. Set aside. Cook the noodles according to the
instructions on the packet. Heat the stock in a large non-stick
pan. When it is bubbling gently, add the mangetout, cabbage, mushrooms, carrots, shallots and peppers and stir-fry
on a high heat for 3 minutes. Add the beansprouts and stir-fry
for 1 minute, then add the sauce, lower the heat and simmer
for 2 minutes. Add the roasted sesame seeds and serve
immediately with the noodles.

Stir-Fried Rice and Vegetables

This Chinese dish will appeal to all tastes, including the
faddy ones of many children. It has such a wonderful flavour
that most people find they want to come back for more.

3 tablespoons vegetable stock
2 cloves garlic, crushed
1 tablespoon grated fresh ginger root, or ½ teaspoon
powdered ginger
3 shallots or small onions, finely chopped
3 medium carrots, finely chopped
1 green pepper, seeded and sliced
1 red pepper, seeded and sliced
8oz (225g) broccoli, finely chopped
2oz (50g) bean sprouts
1 tablespoon soy sauce
2 tablespoons dry sherry
8oz (225g) cooked brown rice
freshly ground black pepper

Preparation time: 10 minutes
Cooking time: 10 minutes

Heat the stock in a large non-stick frying pan and stir-fry
garlic, ginger and shallots for 2 minutes. Add the carrots,
green and red peppers, broccoli and bean sprouts and stir-fry,
lowering the heat slightly, for another 3 minutes. Add the soy
sauce and dry sherry, stirring all the time, then add the
cooked brown rice and continue to stir-fry until heated right
through. Season with pepper and serve immediately.

Brown Rice and Carrots

I'm always falling back on this dish, which is easy and highly
nutritious. It's also a good recipe if you have leftover cooked
rice.

2–3 tablespoons vegetable stock
1 medium onion, finely chopped
8oz (225g) carrots, grated
2–3 courgettes, diced – or you could use 3–4 large
flat mushrooms
8oz (225g) brown rice, cooked
sea salt and freshly ground black pepper
2 tablespoons chopped fresh parsley
3 tablespoons sesame seeds

Preparation time: about 5 minutes
Cooking time: 10 minutes

Heat the vegetable stock in a large saucepan and stir-fry the
onion and grated carrots for a few minutes until soft. Add the
courgettes and continue cooking for a few more minutes,
stirring all the time. Lower the heat, add the rice and stir in.
Add the seasoning, parsley and sesame seeds. When all is
heated through, serve with a mixed or green salad. Creamed
spinach goes well with this dish, and adds welcome dark-
green colour, especially if you use mushrooms.

COOKING WITH TOFU

A totally tasteless cheese-like white block in its natural state,
tofu is a cellulite-shifter's delight. It is low in calories,
dairy-free, highly nutritious, and blends in well with many
kinds of food.

Tofu is easily available at every healthfood shop, it is

cheap and versatile and can increasingly be found in super-markets. It can be used in both savoury and sweet dishes instead of cheese and dairy products.

Tofu-Topped Vegetables

This dish, which is quick and easy to prepare, is popular at dinner parties. I cook it often, and it has been pronounced delicious by people who have never heard of tofu and who would probably turn their noses up at it if you told them what it was. (I'm thinking of the typical meat-and-two-veg un-reconstructed male, who affects to despise 'healthy' food.)

1lb (450g) fresh spinach, or use frozen leaf spinach
½ cup vegetable stock
12oz (350g) white cabbage, shredded
2 leeks, cleaned and chopped
3–4 courgettes, diced
3–4 carrots, diced
2 cloves garlic, crushed
1 teaspoon sea salt
freshly ground black pepper
2 packs tofu – firm, if possible, not silken
3 tablespoons tahini
juice 1 lemon
1 teaspoon soy sauce
4 tablespoons natural low-fat yoghurt, or use
natural soya yoghurt
¼ teaspoon cayenne pepper
2oz (50g) wholemeal breadcrumbs (optional)

Preparation time: 15 minutes
Cooking time: 45–50 minutes

Preheat the oven to 350°F, 180°C, gas mark 4.

Cook the spinach until tender. It's easy to cook spinach – the real problem is getting it free from grit, which is why lazy cooks (like me) tend to use the frozen variety. Fresh, just-washed spinach does not need water adding; just put it all in a pan, bring to the boil and cook over a medium heat for about 5 minutes. You'll be amazed at how quickly fresh spinach boils down to almost nothing.

Heat the stock in a large non-stick pan and stir-fry the cabbage and leeks for 1–2 minutes. Cover, lower the heat and simmer for 4–5 minutes more. Add the courgettes and carrots and stir-fry for 4–5 minutes over a medium heat, then add the garlic and cook for 4 more minutes. Add the cooked spinach to the pan with the sea salt and pepper. Remove from the heat and transfer the contents to a large casserole dish.

In a liquidizer, combine the tofu, tahini, lemon juice, soy sauce, yoghurt and cayenne pepper and liquidize until smooth. Pour over the vegetables and top with the bread-crumbs, if using. Bake for about 35 minutes or until it is slightly browned and bubbling gently.

Serve with salad. Jacket potatoes (see page 102) go well with this dish.

Tofu Shepherd's Pie

This is such an improvement on the traditional version, and it is popular with all age groups and even fussy eaters.

½ cup vegetable stock
1 onion, finely chopped
8oz (225g) mushrooms, chopped
1 green pepper, seeded and sliced
2 large carrots, finely chopped
6 tomatoes, skinned, or 14oz (400g) tin tomatoes, chopped
1 bay leaf
2 heaped teaspoons fresh chopped basil, or
½ teaspoon dried
1 pack Morinaga or Tofeata tofu
sea salt and freshly ground black pepper to taste
1lb (450g) mashed potatoes (do not mash them with butter,
cream or milk)

Preparation time: about 15 minutes
Cooking time: 45 minutes

Preheat the oven to 375°F, 190°C, gas mark 5.

Heat the stock in a non-stick pan, add the onion and stir-fry for 2 minutes. Add the mushrooms, green pepper and carrots and continue to stir-fry over a medium heat for about 3 minutes, then add the tomatoes, bay leaf and basil. Cover and simmer for about 15 minutes.

Chop or break up the tofu and add to the vegetable mixture, stirring all the time. Add the sea salt and black pepper, then turn the mixture into a large casserole and top with the mashed potatoes. Bake in the oven for 20 minutes or until the potatoes are lightly browned.

Serve with a green salad; it doesn't need anything else.

PULSES

Pulses – lentils, black-eyed beans, haricot beans, kidney beans, even baked beans if they are sugar-free – are marvellous foods for those wishing to be rid of cellulite. They provide complex carbohydrates and are nutritionally satisfying, tasty and versatile. I used to soak pulses overnight, but now I've become rather lazy and tend to use those pulses that can be cooked from start to finish in about half an hour, or I use tins. Chick peas and kidney beans tin well, and in recipes it is impossible to tell the difference. Always rinse tinned pulses in filtered water before using, as they tend to be preserved in brine.

However, as it is always useful – and cheaper – to have stocks of dried pulses, this is how to cook them by the quick-soak method rather than soaking overnight. Allow 8oz (225g) pulses for four people. They will swell up to twice their size when cooked.

Haricot beans Put 8oz (225g) beans in a saucepan with 1½ pints (900ml) water, cover and bring to the boil. Simmer for 2 minutes, then turn off the heat. Leave to soak for 2–3 hours, then bring to the boil again, reduce heat and simmer for 2 hours until tender.

Butter beans Soak 8oz (225g) beans overnight in plenty of cold water. The next day, drain, rinse, then put in a pan with 2 pints (1.2l) fresh water. Bring to the boil, reduce heat, and simmer for 3 hours or until tender.

Chick peas Put 8oz (225g) chick peas in a saucepan with 2 pints (1.2l) water, cover and bring to the boil. Simmer for 2 minutes, then turn off the heat and leave to soak for

3 hours. Bring to the boil again and simmer for another 3 hours or until they are very tender.

Black-eyed beans These have the advantage of cooking very quickly without pre-soaking. Bring 8oz (225g) black-eyed beans to the boil in 1 pint (600ml) water, then reduce heat, cover and simmer for 30 minutes or until tender.

Kidney beans These are difficult to cook properly, which is why I always buy tins and drain off the fluid. But for 8oz (225g) beans you need 1 pint (600ml) water. Put the beans in a saucepan with the water and bring to the boil. Cover and simmer for 2 minutes. Let stand for about 3 hours, then bring to the boil again and boil hard for 10 minutes. Reduce the heat and simmer for 1 hour, or until extremely tender.

Aduki beans Put 8oz (225g) aduki beans into a saucepan with 1 pint (600ml) water and bring to the boil. Simmer for 2 minutes, turn off the heat and leave to stand for 1 hour. Bring to the boil again and simmer for 1 hour or until tender.

Red and brown lentils These cook quickly and do not need pre-soaking. Using twice as much water as lentils, bring to the boil and simmer, covered, until cooked and mushy. Red lentils take 30 minutes at most, and brown ones about 45 minutes. Check every now and again that the water has not evaporated, as burned lentils are horrible. While cooking, they can be flavoured with a bay leaf.

Note: if you have a pressure cooker, you can cut down the cooking time considerably. Cook according to the instructions for your model.

For all beans, sea salt can be added towards the end of

the cooking time. This takes out some of the 'windiness' associated with beans.

Lentil Shepherd's Pie

¾ pint (450ml) vegetable stock
1 large onion, finely chopped
1 stick celery, chopped
6oz (175g) red lentils
½ teaspoon yeast extract
½ teaspoon fresh thyme or pinch dried
½ teaspoon fresh sage or pinch dried
6oz (175g) carrots, grated
1lb (450g) potatoes
1 bay leaf
sea salt and freshly ground black pepper
a little low-fat yoghurt or fromage frais

Preparation time: about 20 minutes
Cooking time: about 45 minutes

Heat about 2 tablespoons of the stock in a large non-stick frying pan and stir-fry the onion and celery for about 2 minutes. Add the lentils, remaining stock, yeast extract, thyme, sage and grated carrots and bring to the boil. Simmer for 30 minutes. Meanwhile, scrub potatoes, cut into 2 inch (5cm) pieces, place in a pan with the bay leaf and cover with water. Add 1 teaspoon sea salt and bring to the boil, then simmer for 25 minutes or until tender. Drain, and mash with freshly ground black pepper and a little low-fat yoghurt or fromage frais. Place the lentil mixture in a pie dish and top with the potato. Heat under the grill for about 5 minutes.

Serve with steamed spinach, broccoli or cabbage, or a green salad.

Brown Lentils and Buckwheat Spaghetti

This is an all-time favourite with my family. Most children love it, and don't even realize that there is no meat in it. The only drawback is that it takes rather a long time to cook.

8oz (225g) brown lentils
1 pint (600ml) water
2 bay leaves
sea salt and freshly ground black pepper
1½ pints (900ml) vegetable stock
1 onion, chopped
1 clove garlic, crushed
4 large carrots, chopped
2 sticks celery, chopped
1 dessertspoon tomato purée
4oz (125g) mushrooms, chopped
2–3 tablespoons chopped fresh parsley

Preparation time: 20 minutes
Cooking time: about 1½ hours

Preheat the oven to 400°F, 200°C, gas mark 6.

Put the lentils into a pan with the water, and bay leaves and seasoning. Bring to the boil, cover, then lower the heat and simmer for about 45 minutes, making sure it does not boil dry. You may need to taste from time to time to see if the lentils are cooked – if there is a trace of hardness they need longer.

Meanwhile heat about ¼ pint (150ml) of the stock in a large, non-stick frying pan and stir in the onion and garlic. Stir-fry for about 5 minutes over a medium heat. Stir in the carrots and celery and cook for a few minutes more, then add the tomato purée and the rest of the stock. Bring to the boil, then add the mushrooms, cooked lentils and parsley. Season, then lower the heat and simmer for about 45 minutes. About 10 minutes before the sauce is ready, cook the buckwheat spaghetti according to instructions. Serve topped with the lentil sauce.

Vegetable Casserole

This is a really simple casserole which makes a good weekday supper dish.

8oz (225g) brown lentils
3–4 medium carrots, chopped
2 sticks celery, chopped
2 onions, finely chopped
1 heaped teaspoon each chopped fresh sage and thyme, or
½ teaspoon each dried
1 large cooking apple, cored and chopped
sea salt and freshly ground black pepper
¾ pint (450ml) vegetable stock
1 tablespoon oatflakes

Preparation time: 10 minutes
Cooking time: about 45 minutes

Preheat the oven to 350°F, 180°C, gas mark 4.

Put all the ingredients except the oatflakes into a casserole and cover completely with vegetable stock. Sprinkle over the oatflakes, cover with a tight-fitting lid and bake in the oven for about 45 minutes or until completely cooked.

Lentil and Swede Bake

Many people turn up their noses at swedes, but cooked this way they are delicious and tasty, and quite unlike the mashed tasteless swedes we remember from school dinners.

8oz (225g) red lentils
1 pint (600ml) water
2 bay leaves
sea salt and freshly ground black pepper
8oz (225g) swede, grated
¼ pint (150ml) vegetable stock
1 medium onion, chopped
2 sticks celery, chopped
about ⅛ nutmeg, grated
2 tablespoons chopped fresh parsley
a little olive oil
4 tablespoons wholemeal breadcrumbs

Preparation time: about 20 minutes
Cooking time: 1 hour 20 minutes

Preheat the oven to 400°F, 200°C, gas mark 6.

Put the lentils into a saucepan with the water, bay leaves and seasoning. Bring to the boil, cover and simmer gently for about 40 minutes. Mix in the grated swede and cook for another 10 minutes, by which time all the water should be absorbed. Remove from the heat.

While the lentils are cooking, heat the vegetable stock in a separate pan and cook the onion and celery over a gentle heat until tender – about 15 minutes. Mix into the lentil and swede purée, adding the nutmeg and parsley. Season again to taste, then transfer to an oiled casserole dish – just smear a little olive oil over the surface with a paper towel – and sprinkle over the wholemeal breadcrumbs. Bake in the oven for 30 minutes.

Kidney Bean Casserole

This is a very warming and filling winter dish. As it contains chillies, it is also quite hot. If you are cooking this dish for children or people who don't like very spicy food, omit the chillies and instead use 1 dessertspoon paprika.

8oz (225g) red kidney beans, or 14oz (400g) tin
1 pint (600ml) water, if using dried beans
1lb (450g) tomatoes, skinned and sliced
sea salt and freshly ground black pepper
2 large red peppers, seeded and sliced
2 medium onions, sliced
1 clove garlic, crushed

2 fresh red chillies, seeded and finely chopped, or
2 dried red chillies
2 teaspoons paprika

Preparation time: about 15 minutes
Cooking time: if using tinned beans, 1½ hours; otherwise, about 2½ hours.

If using dried kidney beans, cook them according to the instructions on page 119. Preheat the oven to 325°F, 160°C, gas mark 3.

Layer half the tomatoes in a large casserole, season well, then add a layer of peppers, onions and garlic, chillies and paprika. Put in all the beans, followed by a second layer of peppers, onions and garlic, with the remaining tomatoes on top. Season again. Cover the casserole and bake in the oven for about 1½ hours. Serve with brown rice and a green salad.

Black-eyed Beans with Mixed Vegetables

A very filling and tasty dish. Black-eyed beans cook very quickly and have a creamy taste.

8oz (225g) black-eyed beans
1 pint (600ml) water
about ½ pint (300ml) vegetable stock
1 large onion, sliced
1 clove garlic, crushed
12oz (350g) courgettes, sliced

12oz (350g) tomatoes, skinned and sliced
12oz (350g) flat mushrooms, chopped
1 green pepper, seeded and sliced
sea salt and freshly ground black pepper
1 tablespoon mixed fresh herbs, or 1 teaspoon dried

Preparation time: around 15 minutes
Cooking time: 35–40 minutes

Put the black-eyed beans into a saucepan with the water and bring to the boil. Reduce heat and simmer until tender (about 30 minutes). Meanwhile, heat 2–3 tablespoons of the vegetable stock in a large saucepan and sweat the onions, garlic and courgettes over a medium heat for 5 minutes. Add the remaining vegetables and stock and bring to the boil. Season, add the herbs, then lower the heat and simmer until the vegetables are cooked – about 15 minutes. When the black-eyed beans are ready, stir into the vegetable mixture and check the seasoning. Serve with a green salad and, if liked, jacket potatoes. Brown rice could also accompany this dish.

Vegetable Bake

3 medium onions, chopped
3–4 carrots, diced
2 large old potatoes, peeled and sliced
½ pint (300ml) vegetable stock
2 tablespoons chopped fresh mint, or 2 teaspoons dried

sea salt and freshly ground black pepper
1 tablespoon cold-pressed oil
2 cloves garlic, crushed
2 tablespoons sesame seeds

Preparation time: about 10 minutes
Cooking time: about 45 minutes

Preheat the oven to 400°F, 200°C, gas mark 6.

Put the onions, carrots, potatoes and vegetable stock into a saucepan. Bring to the boil, then lower the heat and simmer for about 15 minutes or until the vegetables are cooked.

Transfer the onions, carrots and any remaining stock to a lightly oiled casserole dish, mixing in the mint and seasoning well. Then arrange the potatoes on top. Brush the oil over the potatoes and sprinkle with the garlic and sesame seeds. Bake in the oven for about 30 minutes or until the potatoes turn golden-brown.

Vegetable Risotto

A colourful and easy dish, complete in itself, which will be popular with all the family.

8oz (225g) brown rice
1 large onion, finely chopped
1 clove garlic, crushed
3 tablespoons vegetable stock
1lb (450g) spinach, washed and chopped

8oz (225g) broccoli, chopped
corn from 1 corn on the cob, or use tinned corn
4oz (125g) cashews (*not* salted or roasted ones)
1 teaspoon fresh or ½ teaspoon dried rosemary
1 teaspoon fresh or ½ teaspoon dried tarragon
about ⅛ nutmeg, grated
pinch powdered cloves
1 tablespoon chopped fresh parsley
sea salt and freshly ground black pepper

Preparation time: 10 minutes
Cooking time: about 40 minutes

Cook the brown rice in lightly salted water. While the rice is simmering, sweat the onion and garlic for about 5 minutes in the vegetable stock over a medium heat. Add the spinach, broccoli, and corn, and stir-fry until the vegetables are tender. Do not allow to burn and stick to the pan. Dry-roast the cashews for a few minutes in a heavy pan over medium heat, stirring all the time.

When the rice is cooked, stir in the vegetables, cashews, herbs, cloves and parsley. Season to taste and heat through very gently. Serve immediately.

Spinach and Noodles

This is extremely quick and easy, provides a fully balanced meal and is enormously popular, in my experience.

8oz (225g) wholemeal noodles or wholemeal macaroni
2lb (900g) spinach, washed and chopped
4oz (125g) cashew nuts
1 sprig rosemary, finely chopped, or ½ teaspoon
dried rosemary
about ⅛ nutmeg, grated
sea salt and freshly ground black pepper
4 tablespoons natural low-fat yoghurt, or plain soya yoghurt
4 tomatoes, skinned and sliced

Preparation time: about 10 minutes
Cooking time: 15 minutes

Cook the noodles or macaroni according to the instructions on the packet. At the same time, cook the spinach for about 10 minutes in only the water that is left after washing. Dry-roast the cashews over a medium heat, stirring until they start to turn brown, then remove at once. Remove the spinach from the saucepan, drain and chop finely. Transfer back to the saucepan, and add the rosemary, nutmeg, salt and pepper. Stir over a low heat for 2 minutes, making sure it does not burn, then add the yoghurt and stir thoroughly until completely heated through. By this time the noodles should be ready. Drain and transfer to a heated serving dish and pile the spinach mixture on top. Arrange the tomatoes over the spinach and serve at once.

Carrot Purée

This is an easy and tasty way of cooking big, old carrots. Serve with jacket potatoes, brown rice or as an accompanying vegetable to a bake or casserole.

¼ pint (150ml) water
4 large carrots, sliced
1½oz (40g) oatbran or finely milled oats
2 fl oz (50ml) skimmed milk or soya milk
sea salt and freshly ground black pepper to taste
½ teaspoon ground cinnamon
about ⅛ nutmeg, grated
2 tablespoons chopped mixed nuts – brazils,
cashews, hazels

Preparation time: 6–7 minutes
Cooking time: 40 minutes

Preheat the oven to 375°F, 190°C, gas mark 5.

Bring the water to the boil, add the carrots and cook quickly until tender – about 10 minutes. Transfer the carrots plus their cooking water to a liquidizer and blend until smooth with all the remaining ingredients except the nuts. Check the seasoning, then transfer to an ovenproof dish, scatter the chopped mixed nuts on top and bake in the oven for 30 minutes.

Special Burgers

Even vegetable burgers can be cooked without using oil or
fat. These burgers have a taste all of their own and are
delicious and filling. Children love them as much as adults
do, and they have the added advantage that they are not soaked
in fat, like ordinary burgers. They are also extremely easy to
make.

8oz (225g) red lentils
1 bay leaf
sea salt and freshly ground black pepper
4oz (125g) mixed nuts (not peanuts), ground
2oz (50g) sunflower seeds, ground
1 medium onion or 2 shallots, chopped and sweated until
soft in a little vegetable stock. Or you could use finely
chopped celery instead
1 tablespoon oatmeal
1 dessertspoon chopped fresh sage or 1 teaspoon dried
few celery seeds (optional)
a little oil for brushing burgers

Preparation time: 10 minutes
Cooking time: 1 hour 10 minutes

Preheat the oven to 400°F, 200°C, gas mark 6.
  Put the lentils in a saucepan with the bay leaf, a little salt
and pepper and twice as much water as lentils. Bring to the
boil, then reduce heat, cover and simmer until a purée is
formed – about 30 minutes. The purée should be fairly

mushy as the burgers will dry out when they are cooked. Check once or twice during cooking that the mixture has not started to stick to the bottom of the pan. When the lentils are cooked, remove the bay leaf.

Mix all the ingredients (except the oil) with the lentil purée in a large mixing bowl and form into burgers. This mixture will make 4–6, depending on size. Lightly oil a baking tray and brush each burger with a little olive or cold-pressed vegetable oil, if you like. This is not essential, but stops the tops from becoming too 'biscuity'. Bake in the oven for 40 minutes, or until slightly browned. Serve with quark or low-fat yoghurt (other members of the family can have sour cream, if they like, or tomato ketchup) and a large salad.

NUT LOAVES

Nut loaves are the vegetarian equivalent of roasts. They are quite time-consuming to prepare and cook, but good for special occasions. All nut loaves can be made in advance and then frozen until needed.

Nut savouries can be made with a huge variety of different nuts, but whatever quantity of nuts you use, you should have an equal amount of cooked brown rice, potatoes or bread-crumbs to act as 'backing'. Otherwise the nuts are too dry and indigestible. You also need flavouring – onions, garlic, shallots, mushrooms, courgettes – and some liquid so that it all coalesces together before you bake. Most nut loaves and savouries take about 40 minutes to bake in a moderate oven. Don't overbake, otherwise they will be dry and biscuity.

Simple Brazil Nut Roast

This is one of the easiest to make. As with all nut loaves, it is very filling. You can use other nuts, such as hazels or cashews, in this basic recipe.

1 large onion, finely chopped
4oz (125g) carrots, grated
about 3 tablespoons vegetable stock
4oz (125g) brazil nuts, finely milled
4oz (125g) wholemeal breadcrumbs
1 teaspoon chopped fresh sage or rosemary or
½ teaspoon dried
sea salt and freshly ground black pepper
3 level tablespoons soya flour
1 tablespoon sesame seeds

Preparation time: 15 minutes
Cooking time: about 45 minutes

Preheat the oven to 350°F, 180°C, gas mark 4.

Sweat the onion and carrots over a medium heat in 2–3 tablespoons vegetable stock for 5 minutes. Add the nuts, breadcrumbs, herbs, seasonings and flour. If the mixture is too dry, add a little more vegetable stock. It should be sticky but not runny. Press into a 1lb (450g) loaf tin and sprinkle with the sesame seeds. Bake in the oven for 30–40 minutes. Serve with salad.

Hazelnut and Tomato Bake

This is a variation on the nut loaf and has been a favourite in my family for many years. It is particularly popular with teenagers.

2–3 tablespoons vegetable stock
1 medium onion, finely chopped
1 clove garlic, crushed
1lb (450g) tomatoes, skinned and chopped
½ tablespoon tomato purée
6oz (175g) hazelnuts, ground
8oz (225g) mashed potato
1 tablespoon chopped fresh parsley
1 teaspoon fresh or ½ teaspoon dried basil
a little olive oil for greasing dish
grated rind ½ lemon
sea salt and freshly ground black pepper

Preparation time: 10 minutes
Cooking time: 40–55 minutes

Preheat the oven to 350°F, 180°C, gas mark 4.

Heat the stock in a large saucepan and cook the onion and garlic for about 5 minutes until softened. Add the tomatoes and boil until reduced in quantity and completely mushy – about 5–10 minutes. Add the tomato purée, remove from the heat and stir in all the remaining ingredients except the olive oil, mixing well. Grease an ovenproof dish with a little olive oil, press in the mixture and bake in the oven for 30–40 minutes. Serve with plain yoghurt and a green salad. This dish is very filling, and a little goes a long way.

CHAPTER TWELVE

FISH AND MEAT MAIN COURSES

This section has been contributed by aromatherapist Frances Clifford, who helped me to get rid of my cellulite.

Meat and fish, says Frances, have very little place in any successful cellulite-shedding regime. The reason is that both these foods clog up the system and putrefy quickly once in the bowel. Also, they do not combine successfully with carbohydrates in the digestive system. Therefore they should be eaten only infrequently – once a week for chicken or other meat, say Sunday lunch, and twice a week for fish. Do not eat animal protein more often than this while you are trying to lose cellulite. Some people do feel better if they eat fish and meat once in a while to gain their full vitamin and amino-acid complement. (Most vegetarians seem to make up the lack without any trouble at all, and few vegetarians are ever found to be grossly deficient in their diet. In fact, it is more likely to be the meat eaters who are deficient.)

When buying meat, make sure it is locally reared, fresh and unprocessed. Do not buy meats that have been extensively processed, smoked, or contain preservatives or additives. Avoid tinned meats, ready-prepared meat meals, bought meat sauces and such dubious delights as hamburgers, fried chicken, doner kebabs and sausages.

Buy meat from a small, independent butcher or from an organization such as the Real Meat Company. Their address is East Hill Farm, Heytesbury, near Warminster, Wilts, BA12 0HR. At the point of sale, meat should be displayed in such a way that air can circulate. The fat should be of a white or creamy colour, with a matt finish. You may find that additive-free, organically produced meat is a paler colour than you have been used to, but that is an indication that no dyes have been added. All meat you buy should smell fresh.

Fish should also be bought as close to its source as possible. Fresh fish is bright-eyed, bright-skinned and not slimy-looking or strange-smelling. Wet-fish counters have now appeared in many supermarkets and these have a quick turnover. Alternatively, find an independent fishmonger where you can check that the fish is freshly caught.

When cooking meat or fish the anti-cellulite way, do not fry or barbecue as very hot cooking oil releases free radicals. It is better to 'dry-roast' meat – that is, put it in a covered pot or casserole with seasonings, and cook on a very low heat (275°F, 140°C, gas mark 1) for several hours. If you have a crockpot, you will find this invaluable, but whatever you do, never fry the meat in oil first.

Small pieces of meat can be grilled under a low to medium heat. The use of aromatic herbs and spices improves the smell of cooking meat and also stimulates the flow of vital digestive juices.

Remember that human beings are not really designed to eat meat, as our colons are too long. A heavy meat diet causes constant putrefaction in the colon and a steady process of autointoxication which eventually adds to the cellulite load. You may also experience feelings of lethargy, bloating and heaviness after eating too much meat or fish – hence the time-honoured nap after Sunday lunch. Frances recommends that if you ever feel heavy after eating meat you should go completely vegetarian for a while.

For those who feel they need some meat or fish in their diet (or who are reluctant to give it up completely) Frances recommends a ninety per cent vegetarian, ten per cent meat or fish diet. This is completely adequate – nobody needs more animal protein than this. Relegate meat and fish to bit-part players instead of assigning them the leading role in your cookery.

Frances attributes her own abundant good health to a diet that contains very few animal products of any kind.

These are Frances's favourite anti-cellulite fish and meat recipes – the ones she recommends to her patients who wish to be rid of their cellulite deposits.

Lemon-baked Plaice

1–2 fillets plaice per person
grated rind ½ lemon and 2 teaspoons lemon juice per fillet
sea salt and freshly ground black pepper
2 dessertspoons mixed fresh herbs – thyme, marjoram,
parsley, oregano, for example – or ½ teaspoon mixed
dried herbs per fillet
lemon wedges and parsley sprigs to garnish

Preparation time: 10 minutes
Cooking time: 40–50 minutes

Preheat the oven to 325°F, 170°C, gas mark 3.

Season each fillet with lemon rind, salt and pepper. Roll each one up and secure with a cocktail stick or skewer. Pack the prepared fillets into a casserole, sprinkle over the mixed herbs, cover with the remaining lemon juice and rind, and cover with a lid.

Cook for about 40–50 minutes, or until the plaice is completely white and flakes easily. When ready, lift out with a fish slice onto a warmed serving dish. Garnish with the lemon wedges and parsley. Serve with a mixed green salad, steamed mangetout and new baby carrots or baby corn.
Note: This recipe can be adapted to any kind of flat fish.

Dinner Party Salmon

1 bay leaf per steak
1 salmon steak per person. Buy wild salmon if possible
about ½ teaspoon extra-virgin olive oil per steak
sea salt and freshly ground black pepper
juice ½ lemon or 1 teaspoon dry martini per steak
1 dessertspoon chopped chives or parsley per salmon steak

Preparation time: 10 minutes
Cooking time: about 20 minutes

Lightly oil a large grill pan with olive oil. Arrange the bay leaves in the pan and place 1 salmon steak on each. Brush the steaks with the olive oil and season with salt and pepper. Cook gently under the grill – the flame should not be turned up high and the steaks must not be allowed to char – to allow natural oils to be released and also so that the bay leaf aroma penetrates each steak.

After about 20 minutes, or when the fish is flaky, pour over the lemon juice or dry martini and replace for a maximum of 1 minute under the grill. Put the steaks on a hot serving plate with the cooking juices, and garnish with chopped chives or parsley. Serve with tossed green salad and mixed steamed vegetables.

This dish can be kept warm in the oven for 30 minutes, on a very low heat, if kept well covered. This gives time for a starter.

Note: this recipe can be used for any fish steaks.

Aromatic Pot-Roast Chicken

Organically reared, free-range chicken smells quite delicious when cooking and produces relatively few juices compared to mass-produced birds that have been plumped up with water and preservatives.

1 organically reared chicken, corn-fed if possible
2–4 garlic cloves, peeled and halved
2 lemon halves, or 1 onion, peeled, with up to
10 cloves pressed into it
extra-virgin olive oil
sea salt and freshly ground black pepper
1 teaspoon dried or 1 dessertspoon fresh tarragon
or rosemary
lemon wedges, fresh herbs, raw onion rings to garnish

Preparation time: 15–20 minutes
Cooking time: 1½–1¾ hours

Preheat the oven to 400°F, 200°C, gas mark 6.

Prepare the chicken by rinsing in cold water inside and out, then dry with a piece of kitchen towel roll. Discard the giblets. Using a sharp pointed knife, make 4–8 deep slits in the fleshiest part of the chicken – thigh or breast – and push the garlic halves well down into these.

Put the lemon halves or the onion inside the chicken. Smear the upper part of the chicken with olive oil and put into a casserole. Season with salt and pepper and tarragon or rosemary. Cover with a lid and cook for 30–45 minutes, then reduce the heat to 300°F, 150°C, gas mark 2 and cook for 1 further hour. Test by sticking a knife in the thigh. If the juices run clear, the chicken is cooked.

To serve, place the chicken on a preheated dish. Remove the lemon or onion and pour the cooking juices over and around the bird. Garnish with lemon wedges and fresh tarragon or a few raw onion rings and sprigs of rosemary.

Serve with steamed carrots and broccoli, and a green salad.

Chicken cooked in this way is also very good cold.

Chicken Roll

This is very similar to the previous recipe and uses the same ingredients. Ask your butcher to bone the chicken for you.

Prepare on a chopping board a mixture of chopped or

crushed garlic cloves, grated lemon rind and green herbs, such as parsley or thyme. Spread the chicken out with the inside facing up, and scatter this mixture all over. Season with sea salt and freshly ground black pepper.

Roll the chicken up carefully and use skewers to keep it in a roll shape. Pot roast as before but increase slow cooking time by 30 minutes, as there are no bones to conduct the heat.

This dish is also very good cold.

Lamb

This is the only other 'everyday' meat that Frances recommends to her patients and even this should be eaten very seldom (about once or twice a month maximum) as it is high in fat and can be indigestible if you are trying to refine your diet. English lamb in season – Easter and early summer – is best because it has been subjected to less handling than imported lamb.

Lamb should be cooked using the 'pot roast' method as with chicken, and can be flavoured with lemon or rosemary. Garlic can be inserted into the meat if desired, and the joint can be seasoned with sea salt and freshly ground pepper.

Game Birds

Game eaten in season is very good and makes a welcome change from other forms of flesh protein. Always try to ensure that the game is wild and has been shot on the wing.

Wild birds are lean and should be cooked slowly to preserve moisture. Duck, guinea fowl, pheasant and quail are all good and may be grilled or spit-roasted. Brush first with a very small amount of olive oil.

Pigeon are best braised on a bed of mixed vegetables, such as leeks and carrots, with a little red wine. Juniper berries are the best seasoning for game birds. Consult standard cookery books for game bird ideas, but always use the pot roast method of cooking. Never fry or barbecue.

CHAPTER THIRTEEN

PUDDINGS

Many people imagine that anyone who is serious about shifting cellulite will have to forego puddings for ever. However, this is not quite true. Although double cream and huge slices of Black Forest gâteau are out – except for the very occasional indulgence – there are ways in which you can end a meal with something satisfyingly sweet. For many of us, life would be bleak indeed without any puddings.

Here are some desserts that will cheer you up and satisfy the longing for something sweet at the end of a meal, without encouraging the dread cellulite to return.

Apricot and Tofu Dessert

Yes, our old friend tofu comes to the rescue here. When testing the recipes for this book I asked two people who happened to be in the house at the time – my cleaning lady and a decorator – to try this dish. Although initially suspicious they both, to their surprise, found that they enjoyed eating it, even though it contained unfamiliar ingredients. You can serve this dessert with confidence at a dinner party.

Although this dish is simple and quick to prepare, it has to be thought about several hours in advance if you are using dried apricots.

4–6oz (125–175g) dried Hunza apricots, soaked overnight
and drained, or use the same quantity fresh apricots
1 pack tofu
juice ½ lemon
4 tablespoons raw sugar or organic honey
2 tablespoons low-fat natural yoghurt or plain soya yoghurt
3–4 tablespoons flaked almonds

Preparation time: 5 minutes
Cooking time: nil

Combine all the ingredients except the almonds in a liquidizer. Blend until smooth, then spoon into 4 glass dishes. Top with the almonds and chill.

Strawberries with Tofu

1lb (450g) strawberries (or you could use raspberries)
1 pack tofu
¼ teaspoon natural vanilla essence
juice 1 lemon
4–5 tablespoons raw sugar or honey

Preparation time: 5 minutes
Cooking time: nil

Put most of the strawberries or raspberries in a liquidizer and blend with all the other ingredients until smooth. Spoon into individual glass dishes and decorate with the remaining fruit. Chill before serving.

Tofu Cheesecake

Yes, you can have cheesecake – so long as you make it like this. As it takes a long time to chill, it is best to make it in the morning, or even the night before you need it.

½ cup rolled oats
½oz (15g) desiccated coconut
½oz (15g) butter
1 pack tofu
2 tablespoons low-fat natural yoghurt
2 tablespoons raw sugar or organic honey
juice and rind ½ orange
½ teaspoon natural vanilla essence
2 teaspoons tahini
pinch sea salt
2–3 tablespoons organic honey
4 tablespoons water
½ teaspoon powdered agar-agar (vegetarian gelling agent, available from healthfood shops)
4oz (125g) fresh or frozen raspberries

Preparation time: 15 minutes
Cooking time: about 40 minutes

Preheat the oven to 350°F, 180°C, gas mark 4.

Mix the oats and coconut together in a bowl. Spread the butter over the bottom of an 8 inch (20cm) flan tin, then sprinkle the oat and coconut mixture over this. Press down and set aside. In a liquidizer, combine the tofu, yoghurt, sugar or honey, orange juice and rind, vanilla essence, tahini and salt. When thoroughly blended, pour into the flan case. In a small pan melt the honey in the water over a medium heat and stir in the agar-agar. Bring to the boil and simmer for about 1 minute. Remove from the heat, stir in the raspberries, and pour over the tofu mixture in the flan case. Bake in the oven for 35 minutes. Leave to cool, then chill for several hours before serving.

Fruit Purée with Muesli Topping

This can be served with nut cream or low-fat yoghurt. Use the tiny Hunza dried apricots. They look unappetizing when dried but are far tastier than the bright-orange, sulphured variety.

4oz (125g) dried Hunza apricots, soaked overnight
4oz (125g) sunflower seeds, ground
1 banana
1 apple
juice ½ lemon
½ teaspoon organic honey

FOR THE TOPPING
4oz (125g) muesli base
2oz (50g) raisins
2oz (50g) flaked almonds
2oz (50g) sunflower seeds
2oz (50g) desiccated coconut
(Or you could use Sunwheel 45 per cent fruit and nut
de luxe muesli instead.)

Preparation time: 10 minutes
Cooking time: 5 minutes

Blend together in a liquidizer the apricots, sunflower seeds, banana, apple, lemon juice and honey, adding a little water if the mixture seems too stiff.

Toast the ingredients for the muesli topping under the grill until slightly browned. This will make it crunchy. Spread the topping over the purée and serve.

Baked Apples

This good old British standby makes a wonderful dessert for cellulite watchers.

1 large cooking apple per person, cored

TO FILL EACH APPLE:
½ tablespoon ground or finely chopped brazil nuts
1 tablespoon sultanas or currants
½ teaspoon ground cinnamon
½ teaspoon ground coriander

Preparation time: 5 minutes
Cooking time: 35 minutes

Preheat the oven to 350°F, 180°C, gas mark 4.

To prevent the apples exploding, cut a ring in the peel round the middle before baking. Stuff with the remaining ingredients then bake in the oven for 35 minutes. Serve with nut cream (see page 152), low-fat yoghurt or soya yoghurt.

Peaches with Sesame Seeds

This makes a change from the usual peaches and cream. Use fresh peaches in season rather than tinned ones.

5oz (150g) sesame seeds
6oz (175g) raisins
1 teaspoon ground cinnamon
4 peaches
1 dessertspoon dry sherry

Preparation time: 10 minutes
Cooking time: 25 minutes

Preheat the oven to 375°F, 190°C, gas mark 5.

Mix together the sesame seeds, raisins and cinnamon. Cut the peaches in half, remove the stones, and fill the holes with the sesame seed mixture. Place in an earthenware ovenproof dish, pour over the sherry and bake for 25 minutes, then serve.

Yoghurt Fool

This can be made with almost any kind of fruit, although soft fruits make the nicest yoghurt fools. You need never buy flavoured or sugared yoghurts again. Always buy the plain, low-fat variety and add your own flavourings.

2 punnets strawberries, raspberries, blackcurrants
or redcurrants
2 cartons low-fat yoghurt or plain soya yoghurt
½ teaspoon honey, or to taste
½ teaspoon natural vanilla essence
chopped nuts to serve (optional)

Preparation time: 5 minutes
Cooking time: nil

Blend everything in a liquidizer until smooth and serve chilled in glasses, topped, if liked, with chopped hazelnuts, brazils, cashews or flaked almonds.

Dried Fruit Compote

This dessert has to be planned several hours in advance, as the dried fruit needs soaking beforehand. It is a very easy dish to make, though. The quantities given below need not be adhered to exactly, and you can substitute other kinds of dried fruit if you wish.

8oz (225g) Hunza apricots
2oz (50g) dried prunes
2oz (50g) dried bananas
2oz (50g) dried figs
2oz (50g) dried apples
2oz (50g) raisins
1 pint (600ml) water
4 whole cloves
2 inch (5cm) stick cinnamon
1 tablespoon apple juice concentrate, or 1 teaspoon
organic honey

Preparation time: (excluding time for soaking fruit) 15 minutes
Cooking time: 30 minutes

Soak the dried fruits overnight in the water with the spices and apple juice concentrate or honey. The next day, transfer to a saucepan and bring to the boil. Reduce the heat and simmer for about 25 minutes. Remove the spices before serving. This compote can be served either hot or cold, on its own or covered with crunchy topping (see page 148). If served hot, it goes down well with low-fat yoghurt or nut cream (see page 152).

No-Cook Cake

This uncooked cake tastes just as good as, if not better than, standard baked cakes.

8oz (225g) oatflakes, fine, coarse or medium – it
doesn't matter
4oz (125g) cashews, brazils or almonds, ground
1 banana, mashed
1 carrot, grated
juice 1 lemon
1 dessertspoon organic honey
water or soya milk to mix
strawberries, raspberries or fresh apricots to garnish

Preparation time: 15 minutes
Cooking time: nil

In a large mixing bowl, combine all the ingredients except
the fruit for garnish, adding just enough water or soya milk –
or you could use ordinary skimmed milk – to make the
mixture moist and sticky. Press into a shallow cake tin,
decorate with fresh fruit and chill for 1–2 hours. Serve with
yoghurt or nut cream (see below).

Nut Cream

All my life I have been a lover of double cream, clotted
cream, top of the milk, tinned cream even. The thicker and
gooier the better. That is, I was until I discovered nut cream
– a healthier and really far nicer kind of cream. Now, I never
buy dairy cream and hardly ever have it when eating out. Nut
creams are nice, and definitely not naughty.

Although very few restaurants make nut creams yet, they

are very easy to make at home and I have found them extremely popular with guests. Nut creams don't taste exactly like dairy creams, but have a delightful taste all of their own. The vanilla essence is not essential, but highly recommended. It must be the real thing, not synthetic.

4oz (125g) cashew nuts or almonds, ground
1 teaspoon natural vanilla extract
¼ pint (150ml) water
½ teaspoon organic honey

Preparation time: about 5 minutes
Cooking time: nil

Put all the ingredients in a liquidizer and blend on high speed until completely smooth. Nut creams taste better if chilled, so keep in the fridge until required.

Carob Cream

Carob, the cellulite watcher's alternative to chocolate, can be used in any recipe that calls for chocolate. I must point out though that as chocolate is such a favourite food, many people find the taste and texture of carob disappointing. I did at first, but now I've got used to the less sweet, more powdery taste and I prefer it. It took a long time, though.

Carob cream can be used instead of ordinary or nut creams, and is good for spooning over fresh fruit. It turns simple fresh fruit into a proper dessert.

2oz (50g) cashew nuts, ground
3 tablespoons carob flour
1 teaspoon natural vanilla essence
1 teaspoon organic honey
a little water

Preparation time: about 5 minutes
Cooking time: nil

Blend all the ingredients together on high speed in a liquidizer until completely smooth. The thickness of the cream will depend on how much water you add. It is best to start off with very little water – say 2 tablespoons – and add as required while the cream is blending.

READY-MADE DESSERTS

If you are an ice-cream lover, look out for dairy-free ice-creams. These are increasingly available and offer a delicious alternative to those made with either dairy ingredients or 'non-milk fat', whatever that may be. They do not taste exactly the same as dairy ice-cream but have a wonderful taste of their own. *Sweet Sensation* is a range of non-dairy, lactose-free frozen desserts. Flavours include raspberry ripple, tutti-frutti, black cherry, and vanilla. *Maranelli's* also make an 'ice supreme' with organic soya milk, in chocolate, vanilla and raspberry flavours. These ices are sweetened with apple juice, not sugar.

Berrydale's make a non-dairy ice-cream in a range of

flavours. The ingredients are tofu, honey, soya milk, apple concentrate and flavouring. These ices are also low in cholesterol and are lactose-free.

Plamil produces a range of soya desserts which do not have to be kept in the fridge.

CHAPTER FOURTEEN

PACKED LUNCHES AND EATING OUT

Although most canteens, school cafeterias and college refectories now serve vegetarian meals, it is still not all that easy to find the right sort of food when you are eating out. Often the only answer is to pack up your own lunch before leaving the house in the mornings.

This does not have to involve lengthy preparations. For example, you can spread hummous on oatcakes or barleycakes, cover with fresh alfalfa sprouts, cucumber or tomatoes, and season with pepper for a wonderful, healthy sandwich.

Any of the dips or spreads in the chapter on starters make very good sandwich spreads. You do not need butter or margarine. Sesame or sunflower seed spread is delicious in a sandwich, especially when tomatoes, lettuce or cucumber are added. You can also chop up into small pieces carrots, green, red and yellow peppers, and broccoli or cauliflower for crudités. You should not wrap sandwiches in tinfoil (aluminium, which we now know is very bad for us) but in clingwrap or old-fashioned greaseproof paper instead. Then add a low-fat yoghurt, an apple, banana or other fruit in season, and you have a perfect packed lunch. A tub of plain cottage cheese or a packet of quark will take care of your protein needs if you want a change from yoghurt.

Whenever possible, drink mineral or filtered water. Try not to buy fizzy drinks, even the low-calorie kind, as they contain all sorts of nasties. Aqua Libra is good but very expensive. Most fruit juices are really too concentrated for the cellulite-watcher so dilute them with mineral water whenever possible.

Most supermarkets now sell ready-prepared fresh salads. Marks and Spencer do a vast range, and although they may seem expensive they often work out cheaper than buying a whole cauliflower or a whole pound of broccoli, for instance, and then not being able to use it all up.

What if you are in a situation where you cannot avoid eating out? Well, obviously once in a while it does no harm to eat a cheese sandwich, an ice-cream composed entirely of artificial ingredients, or a takeaway meal. However, as you proceed with the anti-cellulite diet, you become less and less able to eat junk food. It just tastes horrible, and makes you feel too full and uncomfortable. The more 'good' food you eat, the more refined your system becomes, and the less able to digest artificial or over-sugared or salted foods.

At the time of writing, British Rail is still in the dark ages over food. Although its 'Traveller's Fare' is very extensively advertised, it doesn't suit travellers like me. Even now, there is absolutely nothing I can eat in the dining car, and the 'great British breakfast' or the highly expensive 'Continental' version contains everything a cellulite-watcher should avoid. The buffet car is no better. Occasionally, there are some Granny Smith apples, but otherwise – nothing. It is the same with buffet facilities in the stations – there is just nothing I can eat.

My solution is to pack up something suitable for myself before I travel, because I know for a fact that I will not be able to find anything I can eat either on the train or at the station.

Airports and airlines, by contrast, have improved out of all recognition in the past few years. When flying, I always order the vegan menu about twenty-four hours in advance, and it is usually absolutely delicious. It comes with herbal tea, and also you are served first, to the envy of the other passengers. The vegetarian menu available, so far as I know, on all airlines, is also consistently good in my experience. Most main airports have salad and health bars where you can buy exactly the sort of food you should be eating.

For many of us, eating out at an expensive restaurant is a treat. But expensive restaurants are geared more to gourmets than to providing truly nourishing food. Most high-priced restaurants rely on taste sensations, exotica, complicated sauces, expensive meats – none of which you need. However, I must say that in ten years of being a strict vegetarian I have never experienced any real problem in restaurants. Usually there is a starter or two that is acceptable, and you can always ask for a plate of plain steamed vegetables, or a large salad. Wherever possible avoid steak bars and steak houses, as they often serve only peas or fried mushrooms as vegetables – they too are stuck in the dark ages over food, and imagine that meat has to dominate every plate while the rest of the food is merely a garnish to make the dish look pretty. As a general rule, the more expensive the restaurant, the more likely that they will be able to provide you with a plate of plain vegetables, or plainly cooked fish if you are not vegetarian.

Motorway menus are surprisingly good. A few years ago, motorway cafés were heavily criticized, but I have found that I can always get something suitable to eat at them. Most have extensive salad ranges, and chains like Little Chef have introduced a very acceptable range of vegetarian dishes. Motorway cafés all sell mineral water now, and most have herbal teas as well. When I have to travel long distances on motorways I never worry about getting something suitable to eat en route.

What about dinner parties? Again, it does no harm to indulge in cream sauces or Black Forest gâteau once in a while, but there is really no need, as I see it, to eat food that you don't like or shouldn't be having just because you are a guest in somebody else's house. Very often, older people do not understand vegetarian or healthy cooking.

In these situations I occasionally say to the people concerned that I wouldn't want them to go to all the fuss and worry of trying to prepare something suitable, so if they don't mind I will bring my own food. This practice is increasingly accepted nowadays, as many people are on unusual diets and cannot always expect their host or hostess to prepare something special.

I do not go along with the view that you must eat gratefully what your host or hostess has prepared. If the food does not agree with me then I don't eat it. At parties, receptions, weddings, and other such occasions I have frequently been unable to eat any of the food at all.

The answer is to prepare for this eventuality. If I am going to an occasion where I cannot be sure that there will be something suitable for me to eat, I take something to keep me going – an apple or two, a banana, some nuts, an unsweetened carob bar. You can soon get into the habit of doing this.

Alcoholic drinks are not allowed on the anti-cellulite diet. This is partly because they contain large amounts of sugar in the form of empty calories. But the other, more important aspect is that the body treats alcohol as a poison and starts to attempt to detoxify it as soon as it enters the bloodstream. This means that alcohol adds to the toxic load on the liver, which at its best can detoxify only one unit – that's one glass of sherry, half a pint of lager or a single measure of spirits – in an hour. So if you drink faster than this, excess alcohol will stay in the bloodstream. If it is not detoxified, it will turn to fat and eventually, to cellulite. So it is best avoided, at least on a daily basis.

You should never drink extra-strong lagers, which contain huge amounts of sugar, and ideally you should avoid lager altogether, as well as spirits and fortified wines such as port or sherry. Your system can cope with an occasional glass of champagne or wine, especially if it is organic. In fact, whenever buying wines look for organic labels. These are becoming widely available in supermarkets and wine shops. When drinking champagne, intersperse it with non-fizzy mineral water. If you drink the sparkling kind, you will accumulate too much gas and bloating will result.

I have now spent more than two years on the anti-cellulite diet and have never found eating out a problem. It just takes a little thought, a little adjustment – and then it becomes an automatic part of your life.

INDEX